To Margaret.
For Everything.
Love. J

C000082760

M E Williams

May 2011.

A CLUSTER OF FEATHERS

A CLUSTER OF FEATHERS

Mary E. Williams

Book Guild Publishing
Sussex, England

First published in Great Britain in 2010 by
Book Guild Publishing
Pavilion View
19 New Road
Brighton, BN1 1UF

Copyright © Mary E. Williams 2010

The right of Mary E. Williams to be identified as the author
of this work has been asserted by her in accordance with the
Copyright, Designs and Patents Act 1988.

All rights reserved. No part of this publication may be reproduced,
transmitted, or stored in a retrieval system, in any form or by any means,
without permission in writing from the publisher, nor be otherwise
circulated in any form of binding or cover other than that in
which it is published and without a similar condition
being imposed on the subsequent purchaser.

Typeset in Garamond by Ellipsis Books Ltd, Glasgow

Printed in Great Britain by CPI Antony Rowe

A catalogue record for this book is available from The British Library.

ISBN 978 1 84624 443 8

Contents

Prologue

Dear Great-Grandfather, George William Randle,
Your daughter Mary Elizabeth, my namesake and paternal grand-mother, adored you and spoke at length of your very colourful life as the head of a notable firework firm you inherited from your father, who probably inherited it from his father, for it was established in 1782.

As a small child in the 1920s and 1930s, I listened interestedly and avidly as Gran recalled the happenings of her youth. She was a gifted storyteller, and my eyes shone with wonder as her youth unfolded. Your early death when she was but 19 and the demise of the business a few years later due to mismanagement and embezzlement by a trusted relation clearly left a deep sorrow, and I remember crying along with Granny as the story was told.

Because of these memories I have always felt very close to you, especially as Gran insisted that I was born on your birthday; this was manna to an impressionable and imaginative youngster, and brought the 1850s and 1860s right into our art deco living room. Many of these stories tie up with the historical facts of the day.

It is widely known that the great London sewer and water systems were created because of the sewage contamination of well water and the high incidence of cholera, a water-borne disease.

About 1855 you lost your eldest daughter after she fell down a well and caught cholera. Terrified for the rest of your family, you decreed that beer would be the family drink. Consequently, baby Mary (my Gran) imbibed bitter beer with her mother's milk, and although no alcoholic, became attached to it for the rest of her life.

Throughout my long life, most of it spent in North Wales, I have kept alive my recollection and memories of all Gran's anecdotes, especially at night when sleep eluded me; thus you have always been in my thoughts, but occasionally events have occurred that have brought you and yours vividly into focus. One of these took place around Guy Fawkes Day last November.

My nephew Christopher has the habit of leaving his home in Hertfordshire at four in the morning and knocking on my window in North Wales at about 8.30 a.m., having made the journey quickly and efficiently at that early hour. So one morning last November two loved faces grinned at me when I opened my bedroom curtains to a persistent tap: Chris's and his wife Pat's.

Whilst cooking a full British breakfast, excited family conversation ensued, and Chris happened to mention that he had secured a post arranging all the garden activities for Wandsworth Council, plus the firework displays held during November. I perked up on hearing this and immediately said, 'Chris, did you know your great-great-grandfather had a firework factory beside the River Wandle? He specialised in royal exhibitions, including the lavish conclusion to King Edward and Queen Alexandra's wedding.' Because of this amazing coincidence I wrote a synopsis from my memory of your family, Great-Grandfather, and got a promise from Pat to search the Internet (how can I succinctly explain this modern phenomenon?) for any lurking cousins, plus more information about this colourful corner of our joint history. The response was dynamic, and in a short space of time I received the e-mail address of a very interested lady who is the daughter of a second cousin of mine, a woman I only vaguely knew existed.

Celia is the perfect partner to excavate one's life, a local history student who has a decisively delving mind, and between us we have unearthed in just a few months many gems of your past. She is a descendant of your youngest son, Tiny, who was only eleven when you died.

I feel I must make some mention of the changing world, for in the last 200 years magical and incredible discoveries have made everyday life exciting, but unfortunately fear is always with us, and until that is eradicated, the world is not a better place than it was in your day. In your day, just over 150 years ago, computers and television, along with motorcars and aeroplanes, were twinkles in the eye of their inventors. Modern inventions have changed a woman's life forever, and it is also very refreshing not to be regarded as a second-class citizen even when you are an uneducated person such as I am, who left school at 15. There is no doubt, life is much easier these days, but I doubt if people are any happier. How much of all this you know, dear Great-Grandfather, is just conjecture on my part. I don't even know if you still exist, but in my bones I know you are out there somewhere, along with your daughter and other folk dear to me.

Well, as night is closing in, I must leave you, but will return with another, I hope, enlightening letter in the future.

With much love,

Your unknown and unseen great-granddaughter,

Mary

1

Granny, Mary Elizabeth Randle

My paternal grandmother was born in 1856; her father, George William Randle, was a pyrotechnic artist – in bald words, a firework industrialist. She was one of ten or more children, but half died in infancy.

Her elder sister Maria was only five when she fell down a well and contracted cholera which proved fatal. At that time sewage seeped into wells used for domestic use, and it was because so many Londoners were dying of this malady that the main sewage system was begun in 1859.

My great-grandfather – who I always felt very close to because I was born on his birthday, though he died in 1887, almost 40 years before my arrival into this world in 1924 – inherited his firework factory from his father, and family gossip had it that they originally brought the business over from Ireland, but I have never been able to substantiate this. Apparently he was very successful, and for the first few years of my granny's life, the factory was at Vauxhall, but the very dangerous nature of the enterprise, gunpowder being an essential ingredient, made it imperative to move the factory away from the offices and industries that were sprouting in every direction.

They moved to Wandsworth, a verdant pasture, according to Granny, beside the River Wandle. There were green fields where yellow irises, forget-me-nots and marsh marigolds grew. The magazine where the explosives were kept was placed on an island in the river.

Many, many years after Granny had died, in 1995 to be exact, John, my husband, and I were in Wandsworth where he had some business, and we parked our car outside the Town Hall. Somewhat bored and fed up on my own, I looked about and saw a sign which read 'River Wandle'. Curiosity overcame me and I wandered over only to be met by a dried-up riverbed full of rusty kettles and tin cans. Admittedly, we had had a small heat wave, but I found it very difficult to believe that 120 years ago there had been green countryside in the vicinity. Since 1955, local residents have reclaimed this river; the iron bedsteads and tin kettles have gone, and the river is now fast flowing with freshwater fish swimming happily in the clear water.

The family resided in a large house beside the factory buildings where the fireworks were made. Granny had three sisters, Sarah, Lydia and Rebecca, and two brothers, George and Tiny. I do not know Tiny's real name as Granny only ever referred to him as Tiny, and he, George and Sarah died long before I was born; but I remember Auntie Becky and Auntie Lydia vividly.

Apparently the children were all well educated, some being sent to boarding schools, others taught at home, but all were expected to work in the factory alongside the ordinary workforce, and it was here that my grandmother learnt her pithy language. She didn't swear, but her words were vulgar, dirty and so very, very apt. As I remember she was a bit of a Jekyll and Hyde character. When going out, she dressed to the nines in silks and satins, generally black, and always in true Victorian garb. She crimped her front hair with crimpers; her long, black back hair was usually tied up in a bun. The crimpers were a bit like dinky curlers, but rod-like. She wore these at night, and her front hair when combed out was placed over a felt band and secured with hairpins. Believe me, she looked most regal.

Her everyday clothes were just the opposite – serviceable, plain blouses and skirts topped by a blue calico patterned pinny, and when at home, the crimpers never came out. Once when she was ill they stayed in for a month; unfortunately I was at school when they were finally removed, apparently without mishap, much to my dismay for, childlike, I had expected the hair to be matted and stuck to the metal, rendering Granny bald.

In 1851 the firework factory was singled out for recognition by securing the contract to give firework displays at the Great Exhibition in Hyde Park. I know this for a fact because I found several posters of this event, advertising my great-grandfather's business, in a desk of Granny's. Unfortunately, the desk and posters were destroyed by the bomb that hit us during the Second World War.

When I was a small child watching firework rockets explode in the sky, Granny turned to me and said, 'My father isolated the blue firework.' Apparently all the large pyrotechnic firms had been working to make a blue firework; every other colour had been identified, but the blue eluded them until my great-grandfather came up with the winning formula.

In spite of spending gruelling days in the factory, the girls enjoyed a very good social lifestyle. They had music and dancing lessons and possessed up-to-date wardrobes. Their mother, Sarah née Biggs, ran the large house with several servants who, contrary to the standards of the day, ate with the family in the large kitchen. Foodstuffs were ordered in bulk and arrived in large chests.

When Gran, the eldest surviving daughter, was 21, her father held a ball for her; it was a fancy-dress ball, and she was to be a flower seller with a tray of exotic flowers. Everyone wore masks, and Granny, who was an excellent dancer, wanted to make sure that her favourite partner knew who she was, so she asked him in a whisper about his costume. 'Mephistopheles,' he said with a wink, and it was arranged that Gran, who would not divulge her identity, would give him a white camellia. I love that story. I have a white camellia shrub in my garden here as I write in 2009, and it always reminds me of 130-odd years ago, and my dearest grandmother's early years.

At that time the lighting and special effects in the London theatres were dealt with by the firework concerns, and Granny's brothers attended nightly. Just occasionally it was necessary for one of the girls to go instead, and walking back to Wandsworth late at night in the 1880s was a very risky business for a reasonably refined lady, for that was the time of Jack the Ripper, whose main aim was to kill wayward ladies. At that time Gran was married to Grandfather, Henry Kent Hayes (a gentleman who on his paternal side was Irish), but helped out when needed. She said that, although her garb was unlike that of the ladies of the night, the roads were dark and she was very thankful to reach the sanctuary of home.

One night on returning from a stint at a theatre, Gran's brothers approached Westminster Bridge and suddenly stopped. One, with the family twinkle in his eye, suggested that it would be great fun to give the impression that the bridge was on fire. As the play had closed that night they were carrying all their equipment, amongst which was a powder that when ignited gave off huge flames. Although quite terrifying to see, they were quite harmless and died down immediately without damaging the surroundings. Apparently this was used quite extensively for tragic plays.

That night the pair laid the powder along the parapet on one side of the bridge and down the steps onto the embankment by St Thomas's Hospital, where it was lit by a slow match. They then walked quickly in the direction of Old Lambeth Bridge, which was a wooden footbridge in those days, and on looking back saw Westminster Bridge engulfed in flames.

Apparently a lurid description of this mysterious and frightening fire appeared in next day's papers. Luckily the culprits were never found.

As I have mentioned, my great-grandfather George William Randle inherited the family business from his father, who bore the same name. Apparently his firm had enjoyed an enviable reputation from the Regency era, for he exhibited at the Royal Yacht Club, the then famous Vauxhall and Cremone Gardens, and other notable institutions. He was also responsible for the pyrotechnics at the wedding of the then Prince of Wales, later King Edward VII, to Princess Alexandria.

Unfortunately, the second W.G. Randle died when he was barely 50, and his widow carried on the business under the auspices of a good foreman and her young sons. But due to unscrupulousness on the part of someone she trusted, the business fell apart and was finally sold.

Another anecdote of note was the subject of fire in the factory; apparently the substances when used and mixed were very unstable and often resulted in small fires. Water buckets were placed at strategic intervals around the workbenches, and all outbreaks were immediately extinguished. There is no family record of any large fire occurring at the Randle factory. However, the workers often suffered burns, and for this a large bottle of Carron oil was kept to hand. Developed at the Carron Iron Works in Scotland, this lotion was a combination of linseed oil and lime water, and Granny assured me it was the best method to ensure quick healing.

I have tried to impart as factually as possible all Granny's stories as told to a wide-eyed young grandchild. However, the relating took place 70-odd years ago, about events that happened at least 50 years earlier. Some events were substantiated by a few notes my father made, but most are haunting, wonderful memories of mine.

2

Granny's Buttonhook

My grandmother married my grandfather in the 1880s, and my Uncle Frank was born within the year. But Dad didn't arrive until some years later and, owing to poor medication, my grandfather Henry Kent Hayes died after a brief lung illness when Dad was only three.

I only know that he came from an impoverished Irish family who emigrated to England; there must have been some money because Henry was educated at Dulwich College and the Slade School of Art. He made a precarious living, writing for the law courts – remember this was the era before typewriters. All the writing was on parchment and in an ornate style or so Granny said, and when the law courts were sitting, he worked night and day.

He was an innovative man, but his schemes often became hair-raising. One day when he was babysitting Dad and his elder brother Frank, being bored, he decided to pluck the chicken – but hadn't the slightest idea how to do it. When Granny returned, she was met by a snowstorm of feathers, and she couldn't see the two boys. When she did, she was horrified, for Dad's new black velvet suit was covered in down.

Another tale again involved boredom whilst babysitting. He decided the wooden floor was dull and needed a quick polish, so he painted it with some gum he used in conjunction with his work.

When Granny came in her feet stuck to the floor and came up when lifted with a loud glug, glug.

He sounded a most delightful man, and I always regretted not knowing him. His background was very lurid and sketchy. Apparently his father, Timothy Hayes, was a silk merchant based in Paris whose business folded violently, and he took his life by means of a lavatory chain. Poor man, how I have wondered about him; after all, I am of his blood. Why did he do it? Had he in his efforts to keep his business alive acted fraudulently? As they say, his secrets have gone to the grave with him and, although we are a somewhat tragic family, none of his issue have been driven to that dreadful end.

When Henry Kent died, Granny moved back to Wandsworth to be near her sisters, and the two boys grew up there. Money was practically non-existent, and there was no state help of any kind in those days. But compared with many she was lucky, for the house was rented from her brother and his wife. Another bonus came from her husband's first cousin who was wealthy. She allowed Gran an annuity of £3 a month for life, gave numerous gifts to my father and his brother, and paid for their annual holiday. These gifts continued after I and my two brothers were born. Gran said our benefactor used to open grand bazaars and church fetes and send the articles she bought to us. Unfortunately, as I got older I wasn't very grateful for the largesse; I remember Father chasing me round the block because I wouldn't wear a quite presentable dress. I hated the patronage. We never saw her, and Gran never called her by her Christian name, which I believe was Emma. To us all she was Mrs Mac.

These days, £3 doesn't sound much but in the early 1900s it was quite a presentable sum, and Granny augmented it by taking in lodgers.

The boys grew up, and Frank, who had been through an apprenticeship with one of the old railway companies, entailing a stint in

12

every department including the drawing office, was unable after the First World War to get a decent job. So in 1920 he obtained a job as a stationmaster on the British-owned railways in Argentina.

Father took up clerical work and, after serving in the war, left the bank he had worked in since leaving school, and became a company registrar. Gran then left Wandsworth, took a small cottage in Surbiton, and Father commuted daily to town. I and my two brothers, John and Bill, christened William, were born in that cottage and enjoyed a very happy childhood. Our mother was from the West Country and, so everyone told me, was a very beautiful girl.

Gran was certainly a character, used to drinking beer from a very early age, as the water in London was very unsafe until the sewage system was installed. She continued this habit until her death in 1939 at the age of 82.

She was to be seen twice daily at eleven in the morning and six in the evening, draped in an ornate red woollen shawl – a gift from Mrs Mac – with a jug in her hand, walking to the nearest pub to get a pint of bitter. This ritual continued, rain or shine; a Victorian figure in the heart of flapper land, for Surbiton in the 1920s and 1930s was considered to be the 'Queen of the London suburbs'. Because of this, building sites were everywhere, and Granny passed one on her daily 'pub crawl'.

One day she espied a very large boy kicking a very small boy, and saw that the small boy was Bill, her youngest grandson. Disregarding her fragile frame, she took the lout by the shoulder and shook him violently. He reacted and sent the old lady flying into a pile of building sand, thus feeding the sand with her precious pint. The unknown bully fled. Passers-by helped Gran to her feet and took her home. Would she have been prosecuted under today's law? It is likely, for the lad was the only son of a single mother who, having found out our address, turned up that night to threaten Gran with the then existing law. Father tried reason, then ordered her off our property. A month or so later when I was on my way home after school, a strange woman accosted me, held me firmly by the arm, and threatened to beat me because my grandmother had hit her son. With a sudden upward movement, I freed myself and took to my heels. The upshot of this was Gran's failing health; that fall seemed to be a turning point in her life, and gradually she weakened until her death early in 1939.

One of the delights of my early life was to creep into Granny's bed, sink into her deep feather mattress and, in blissful comfort, watch her dress. It took the best part of an hour; how she managed when she was younger and her boys attended school, I do not know.

First she washed in the basin on the washstand. This was cursory, as she wasn't partial to water. I remember Dad coming in one day and, seeing a grubby foot protruding from a mound of bedclothes, shouting, 'Mother! When did you last wash that foot?'

Washing concluded, the real spectacle started. A soft fine common camisole, exquisitely embroidered, was pulled over her old, sagging chest. No bra, just the camisole, then in winter a thick woolly vest, and in summer, a light cotton affair. Then the *pièce de résistance*, a pair of combs – a thin woolly combination garment that was pulled up over her legs. Next, a pink corset complete with bones and long cord ties which were pulled tight over her extremely thin scraggy body that never in its long life had needed a corset, but was tortured because fashion dictated it.

A body warmer was then installed: this article was a 1-foot-square piece of flat quilted material that she placed on her back and tied round her waist; she said it was essential to keep her back warm. Her sister, my Great-Aunt Lydia, had a variation on this theme – her body warmer was 12 inches long but only 3 inches wide, and very much thicker. It looked most uncomfortable, but I was assured that it was a most successful body warmer. Two petticoats then ensued, a full-length cotton affair, and a red flannel beauty, half-size with elasticated waist.

The stockings, lisle for summer, wool for winter, of various dark shades were fastened by suspenders attached to her corset, but for added support, a smart ornate pair of garters graced the tops of her legs. Her bloomers were large, very large, and always colourful. This item concluded the underwear section.

Her everyday top garments usually consisted of a blouse and skirt, the blouses more often than not of Victorian vintage. One that I loved was collarless with black stripes, and she wore it with a cameo of her mother at her throat. A pair of black patent shoes completed the outfit, which in winter was augmented by a pair of leather gaiters fastened by a myriad of tiny buttons. These necessitated the use of a buttonhook, a long, ivory engraved stick with a hook on the end.

I was generally pressed into use to wield the button stick and fasten the buttons by inserting the hook into the buttonhole, hooking the button, and pulling it through the small hole. There were at least 25 buttons on each gaiter, and my hands ached intolerably at the end of the task. But Gran would emerge, and march downstairs triumphant.

She had many satin and silk dresses, most of which were Mrs Mac's cast-offs. They were very rich and opulent-looking even to a child, but the cut and style were of a bygone age. They were truly Victorian. In the 1920s there was a huge gap between the old and young. My mother wore flapper dresses, and Granny and her ilk wore the garments of the old Queen. Today old people wear trousers and are to be seen in summer with large expanses of bare skin.

My mother and Gran got on very well; Gran, who was a first-class cook, prepared most of the food except cakes and pastries, which my mother made to perfection. When Father married her in 1923, she had left her native Cheltenham and was the manageress of a catering establishment in Surbiton. They were so different, but together with Dad, they imparted to us children so much useful information that even today, around 80 years later, I say, 'Where did I learn that?' and it was either from my early school years, or from my home environment.

To bring to an end the memories of my gran I have one incident truly descriptive of the age, which in a way had a pathos to it, but was oh! so gloriously hilarious. When I was about eight some of my friends were attending dancing and recitation classes, but I knew that Dad, who had lost his job in the slump, plus a small business he had started, just couldn't afford that kind of fee. One evening, like children often do, I sat brooding over this, and my mother saw me and I tearfully and selfishly told her. The upshot was, that a distant cousin of Father's who ran a similar establishment, would take me for nothing, as I showed an aptitude for recitation. Oh! but there was one big snag: Joyce's school was 6 miles away in Richmond, could the bus fare be found?

The answer was yes, and I attended regularly. One Saturday morning Dad came with me to visit Joyce's father, who was a favourite relative. We went on the bus, but as it was a nice day, we decided to walk home. Actually Father didn't have the bus money, so we had no option. We enjoyed the walk. At that time there was a discarded First World War cannon on Ham Common, and another outside Kingston Library. Father explained about the construction and the metals used and all in all we had a pleasurable morning, but the bubble burst when we arrived home.

We were late for dinner, and Mum and Gran accused Dad of going into a pub and leaving me outside. They were beside themselves. They just would not believe either of us. This went on throughout the meal until both women were at fever pitch. Granny suddenly disappeared into the outhouse and came back with a large cleaver, which she held above Dad's head.

'I'll cleave you,' she said.

'I'd put that down if I was you,' said Father. 'You might hurt yourself.'

I think this sort of incident was typical of the times, as the slump hit most families, money was scarce, or as in our case, non-existent, for Father had had a well-paid job and was classed as a white-collar worker and didn't qualify for the often-despised dole, a forerunner of today's unemployment benefits. After his business went bust we had nothing but Granny's small pension, Mrs Mac's annuity and her very helpful largesse. Eventually through contacts in the city he obtained a lot of temporary clerking, and we were able to manage.

One other occurrence happened when I was about 12; just then we were quite affluent, Father having found temporary employment. With a little extra money we had a party with a family of friends. We children were playing in the parlour when a knock came at the front door. A gentleman stood there, whom I had never seen before. 'Is your father in?' he asked, so I fetched Father from the kitchen. The man had a sorry tale to tell; he was only slightly known to Father, but had come to us after uselessly canvassing more wealthy friends.

His name was Joseph Novarro, and during the First World War he had been a successful aeroplane designer with his own business, but the slump hit everybody and he had lost everything. Now he was – to use the idiom of the times – flat broke, and was due to be evicted from his flat on the following Monday. Could Father take him and his wife into our home? We lived in a small cottage with tiny rooms and already six people were squashed into its confines. Father had no hesitation in saying yes, so for nearly two years I slept on a made-up bed on the floor of my parents' bedroom. Its mattress was a cast-off featherbed of Granny's, and with complete ecstasy I sank into it. I didn't mind if the Novarros stayed forever.

They stayed until the powers-that-be felt a vague rumbling from

Europe and started to enlarge the aircraft industry slightly. Mr Novarro then got a job as a draughtsman at a local factory and moved into a nearby bungalow.

Although we didn't have much, our parents took us out a bit, sometimes to the London museums where my brothers wallowed in all the latest techniques and ran from exhibit to exhibit in the usual happy childish manner. For me it was the countryside, and I loved every minute we spent picnicking, picking mushrooms, blackberries and wildflowers.

Those years with Gran and my parents were halcyon days. Now in 2009 with hindsight I realise how very necessary a happy, stable childhood is. My feisty, stubborn, eccentric old grandmother gave an extra dimension to my life that would have been missing if she had not been living with our family. In spite of few material comforts, that early period was a diamond time.

3

Schooldays

My first school would today be classed as a hovel; it was one of thousands up and down the country built by the church to educate the poor. In almost every school, the children were cowed and abused, and the nervous lost every shred of confidence. Funnily enough, from my experience in the late 1920s and early 1930s, bullying, although existing, was nowhere near the problem it is today. The building itself, built in 1856, had passed its sell-by date. It was typically Victorian and was situated in the heart of Surbiton and was known (and I believe still is) as St Mark's and St Andrew's Church of England School. But it is now housed in up-to-date modern buildings.

In my day there were three buildings: boys, girls and infants. The boys' had a high-walled playground and was entirely separate from the girls' and infants' buildings which shared a common playground. The outside toilets were very primitive and often overflowed. The three buildings shared a caretaker who was responsible for the overall cleanliness and the fires. The infants were housed in one long room containing two classes and two smaller classrooms. The layout of the girls' school was the same, although the rooms were larger.

In June 1929 I was five, and in the September I was going to school. I can remember the awe, wonderment and fear of it all even now. In those days school dinners hadn't been invented, and I and my neighbour friends walked the half-mile which separated our homes from the school, four times a day. As I was the eldest child, my starting school was an auspicious occasion for Mum and Gran. I had new clothes – no uniform in those days – and my lunch, to be eaten at the 10.30 break, consisted of two biscuits and an apple, tied up in a paper bag.

The teacher was a Miss Lamb, young, dedicated and, I now realise, extremely clever. Every lesson was interesting, and the three R's were interspersed with play-acting, drawing and cutting out. Looking back I realise that the method used in those days to teach children to read was eminently suitable for my highly strung, nervous constitution. We learned by rote: Miss Lamb held up a large board with an object on it and corresponding capital letters, e.g., 'A' for Apple, 'C' for Cat, and in unison we chorused the phonetic sound, and in this impersonal way, I imbibed all the necessary points to become an avid reader. In a few months I was reading everything I could lay my hands on.

I realised how lucky I was when my three children were taught to read by the one-to-one method, and I couldn't understand why, when after two or three years they still couldn't read fluently. My youngest son, Richard, enlightened me when he was a grown man; he was, as a young child, of an extremely nervous and highly strung nature, and the teacher standing over him disturbed him so much that he couldn't concentrate: and it was years before he mastered the art of reading. Gwena, my eldest child, also had difficulty with reading, and I now realise they would have benefited from the class method of reading, for their touchy and sensitive egos would have gained confidence from the rest of the class.

The same condition must have affected my eldest son, Hugh, but he was luckier, for when he was about eight, during a bout of whooping cough, I read aloud to him and Richard, five years his junior, Arthur Ransome's *Swallows and Amazons*, a favourite childhood book of mine. Leaving them while I made my husband's evening meal, I returned to find Hugh deep in the book, reading avidly. Like me, books have become his life blood.

Every day was enjoyable, but I soon came to realise that figures and their usage were meaningless to me; words, on the other hand, were an open sesame to the entire universe – past and present – but working out how much water it would take to fill a bath filled me with horror, and still does 75 years later.

Behind the school were two small shops that sold sweets and other childhood treasures such as marbles, tops, hoops and crayons. I was forbidden to enter one of them, for my mother had seen a large black cat sitting in the window on top of a box of lollipops. Needless to say, I did pop in for the odd sweet after swearing my friends to secrecy.

Playground games soon became an important part of early school life, many of which have disappeared, although I am assured that tag and hide-and-seek are still popular. We had a singular method to select the chaser when playing a game of tag. Five or six of us would huddle in a circle and one girl would count us out, while half-singing a rhyme. There were many different rhymes, most I can't remember, but one favourite one began, 'Have a cigarette, sir. No, sir. Why, sir? Because it makes me cough, one, two, three, out you go.' And that child was 'It' or the chaser, until she or he was fortunate enough to catch another child.

Another favourite game of mine involved a tennis ball being thrown against a solid brick wall; between each throw an action was performed, such as turning around, or passing the ball around the body or under an arm or leg. There was a strict pattern for this game and the divisions were called 'Onesy', 'Twosy', 'Threesy', 'Foursy', 'Fivesy' and Sixy'. In Onesy each action was performed once, in Twosy, twice, and Threesy, three times, and so on up to Sixy, the object being to refrain from dropping the ball. If the game was played with two or more children, as soon as the first player dropped the ball it was the second child's turn until she was hapless enough to misplace the ball. The aim was to go through the whole sequence. Each game possessed five or six different set actions, and some of my older friends were so adept that a ball was seldom dropped. Who first invented this game I have no idea, but it was fairly intricate, and each particular throw was memorised and strictly adhered to. I soon found that this game could be played on one's own, and being an only girl with two brothers, I spent many a summer evening throwing a ball against the high brick wall that separated us from another set of cottages.

When I was very young, a family of four girls and two boys lived next door and the two families were very close. Unfortunately, they moved away when I was seven, and I was bereft of company. The two elder girls, Peggy and Betty, spoilt and mothered me, and it was they who taught me the ball game and other interesting pastimes. One of these involved threading tiny, tiny beads onto thin wire to make brooches in the shapes of butterflies, birds and flowers, plus necklaces woven to create varied and startling patterns. I was never very good at this, or indeed anything that required intricate handiwork.

I remember one afternoon at school at about that time. We were being taught to knit, and all the other girls had neat knitted squares, whilst mine was a minefield of dropped stitches and hanging woollen thread. Our headmistress looked at me, held the offending square up for the class to see, and said with a twinkle in her eye, 'Mary, it's a good thing you won't have to rely on your hands for your living.'

One of the greatest influences of my young life was Surbiton Library. My mother, who was an avid reader of travel books and tomes about foreign lands, visited the old Army hut that housed the original library at least twice a week. When I was about seven a fine new building was built with a large room set aside for children. It was with great dismay that I learnt it was not possible to enjoy the delights of this room until I was nine; meanwhile I devoured all of my mother's collection of books, including most of Dickens and Walter Scott. There was one very trite book called *Eric or Little by Little*. Today I cannot remember the author or contents but recall that after one chapter it was discarded as rubbish. At last my ninth birthday arrived, and armed with the entry form duly signed by my mother, I entered the cherished room.

The librarian at that time was a young, go-ahead girl who held functions on most days of the week. There was a book club and a stamp club, to name but two. There were others, but I only vaguely remember them. Another gem thought up by this ambitious girl was the quarterly magazine, with the cover designed by me. I was also a regular contributor, with lurid stories and poems. Many, many happy hours I spent browsing and delving into the well-filled bookshelves. I could never wait to read my books and would read them as I walked home. Once home and in bed, I would read until the daylight gave up, often hanging out of the window to get the last shred of light. Using the electric light was taboo, for my parents' coffers could not afford even the slightest luxury.

Apart from reading, my other childhood delight was to visit the country. When I was a small child the fields were just around the corner, but by the time I was ten, ribbon development had completely surrounded Surbiton and Tolworth, and at least a 2-mile walk was required before a decent field could be reached. But what joy to revel in a field of buttercups and sorrel, and pick handfuls to present to Mother on our return.

Today children have all the synthetic pleasures of the modern world, but are they as happy and carefree as I was with only a book to read and two healthy feet to traverse town and country alike?

4

To Be or Not To Be

My other grandmother, my mother's mother, Frances Elizabeth Organ, was a showgirl – or should have been, for she was a leading light in an amateur theatrical company when she was 50-plus. She had recited all her life, and in her early thirties her acting abilities had been commented on by leaders of the acting profession.

In real life she was a seamstress before she married my grandfather, Mr J.E. Whittaker, after which she, like all that generation, became a full-time mum and bottle washer. Being a bit of a bright young thing, she had played the field and was engaged four times before JEW, who wouldn't buy her an engagement ring until after they were married.

She had a sister Julia and a brother Charles, and in the records there is evidence of another sister, but neither Grandma nor Mum ever spoke of her. Julia married a Midlands man, and Charles disappeared.

Frances, known as Lizzie, was born in Gloucestershire and lived her entire life there, mostly in Cheltenham. She had the most graphic Gloucestershire accent, laced with honey and cream, and was a very discerning old lady, very sure of herself and quite certain that she was a cut above everybody else. She was always perfectly turned out, with a face that spoke of beauty even at 80.

Her father's name was Merryman Organ. About 20 years ago

when my grandson was ten, one of his school homework subjects was the family tree, and when I told him about Merryman, he refused to include the name in his project. He laughingly said I was pulling his leg, and there was no way I could convince him I was telling the truth.

Merryman Organ at one time was a coachman to a gentleman called Sir William Edge who possessed an estate on the outskirts of Cheltenham. Sir William bred greyhounds, and Merryman was his blue-eyed boy who tended and trained them. One such dog won the Waterloo Cup, but which year, and what dog, I know not. Unfortunately neither Merryman nor his wife Jane (née Vizard) could read or write; I have a certificate signed by each of them with an 'X'. On the other hand their daughter, my grandmother Lizzie, had a fine hand and read copiously, a trait she passed to her daughter Alice, my mother.

When you go delving deep into grass roots, unpalatable facts emerge; my daughter found out that Merryman's father, also called Merryman Organ, was gaoled for stealing wheat to feed his family. I have every sympathy with him, and just thank God that I and my family do not live in such a perilous climate. But what did my very correct grandmother think? Did she know? If so, I never heard of it.

Great-Grandfather Merryman died before my mother was born in 1898, but his wife Jane lived with daughter Lizzie for the remainder of her life. Grandma Lizzie had three children: my mother Alice, her sister Eva and brother Edward. Their father, John Edward Whittaker, was an insurance supervisor and together with Grandmother Jane, they all lived very comfortably, owning their own house, affording a young servant girl, and renting a second home in the country – which sounds grand, but was only a two-roomed cottage.

My mother was very fond of her grandmother. The old lady was a very good storyteller, and one family tale has intrigued me and my family for years. She insisted that the Vizards were, as she put it, 'of Shakespeare's line'. Well, we have dug deep to find some authentication to this statement but can discover nothing concrete. Recently, on the Internet, my daughter Gwena came into contact with the son of a second cousin of mine, one Alan Organ, who was descended from my long-lost grandmother Lizzie's brother Charles who had settled in the Coventry area. Alan, too, had heard of the Shakespeare myth but, again, could find nothing to link our family to the great bard.

Alice, my mother, left Cheltenham for good when she married my father, George Hayes, in 1923 and came to live in Surbiton.

5

Bezique, Shrapnel and Stitches

Surbiton in the 1920s and 1930s was a sleepy London suburb, a peaceful cocoon, when Churchill began striving to awaken the government to the very real threat of Naziism. The whole place was peaceful, even the traffic moved gracefully, whilst the streets and houses yelled affluence from the rooftops. The only happening of any note occurred in the mid-1930s. In the middle of the main shopping street stood a very old shop with a large metal key as a nameplate. We children loved that key. 'Race you to the key' was a favourite pastime.

An old man kept the shop but little was known of him until he was murdered when I was 14. Surprisingly, this did little to upset the equilibrium of the place, even when a picture of the murderer, who was young and handsome, was published. Apparently the old man had been a 'fence' – a wily individual, a middleman who sold stolen goods. As soon as the culprit was hanged, Surbiton returned to its man-less tranquil daytimes, and only slightly awoke in the evenings when the men returned from the city.

No one wanted war; the 1914–18 war had been a very painful experience and life, now that the slump was receding, was good. But as Abraham Lincoln said, 'You can't fool all of the people all of the time', and with Jewish refugees on the streets and gossip percolating as only gossip will, the people knew just what was happening in Germany and that war was inescapable. They were quietly with Churchill all the way.

When war was actually declared amid the hoo-ha of collecting gas masks and identity cards, the fear receded a little. But as Hitler annexed nation after nation, it wasn't easy to go about ordinary daily tasks. People with Jewish blood were extremely jumpy. My family were very apprehensive, for at least one – if not two – of my paternal grandmother's ancestors were practising Jews, and Hitler was eerily planning to punish, torture and exterminate every living person who had one drop of Hebrew blood. One friend with a hint of Jew in his make-up threatened to kill his whole family if we were invaded.

The phoney war continued until the spring of 1940 when the vulnerability of Belgium became obvious, and Dunkirk happened overnight. Amid all this anxiety Churchill took the helm, and we opened our hearts to him. I know the term 'rock' has been over-used during later years, but Churchill was our rock. From then on the fear of invasion lessened, and we, the hoi polloi, never wavered in our devotion to him and our righteous cause. Morale rose from then on, and I personally never knew one person who honestly believed the Hun would win. We were behind Churchill and, in my opinion, any historian who states that the ordinary man thought Britain would be conquered is wrong. I was only a teenager at the time, but I remember. A surge of devotion and courage emanated from the nation when our beloved Bulldog took the reins, and this euphoria lasted until the end of the war when we licked our wounds, cried over our dead, and got on with life once again.

It was soon after the phoney war that the Battle of Britain started and, against incredible odds, we fought off the threat of invasion and convinced Hitler that Britain was a no-go area. The women fed the nation on fresh air and potatoes while the older men, many of whom had served in the First World War, travelled daily on disrupted trains and held jobs of national importance in the city. They not only commuted daily, they manned wardens' posts, fought fires and trained hard with 'Dad's Army', all this with very little sleep.

When the Nazi bombers took over in September 1940, morale was high, and the people, stoic as ever, trudged to the shelters where their comic humour defied all Hitler's hellfire.

This was the time when the war hit me in the gut.

At that time we lived in the house I was born in – the end cottage of a row of six, reached by three footpaths. My father was city fodder and travelled daily; Mum tended myself and my brothers John, 13, and Billy, nine.

The night raids started in mid-September and by the last Sunday of the month had been raging for three weeks. We used the Anderson shelter nightly (a corrugated shed, half-buried). The guns and distant bombs made a lot of noise, but nothing fell locally. Father, a First World War veteran, did a nightly stint at the local wardens' post, and stalwartly attempted to reach his desk each day. Every morning there were large fires, and frighteningly red skies hung low over London; Father reported carnage in the city.

Sunday 29th September was a dull, dark day. Billy, who like all small boys collected conkers at this time of year, had a new pastime gathering shrapnel – great ugly jagged, glinting pieces that cruelly pierced the paper bag that held them. I shuddered; it needed but one small piece to kill a man. As the day wore on the fear that was the night gripped us all. We three children now slept in the downstairs parlour for safety: the powers-that-be emphasised that sleeping in a cellar or on the ground floor was wiser than sleeping in our beds. So be it. John was on the sofa, Bill and I in small beds in the alcove by the fireplace. Mum had deemed the shelter unfit for long-term use. At about six o'clock Father went out; we three bathed in turn in front of the kitchen fire, for we had no bathroom, and then the boys went to bed.

31

Mother and I played Bezique, a card game we particularly enjoyed, but that was the last time I ever played this rather unusual game. About 8.30 p.m. the siren shrieked, but we continued with the game whilst the planes drummed and droned death messages high in the sky, and the guns poured red-hot lethal metal everywhere.

At 9.30 p.m. I was sent to bed, but couldn't settle, which was unusual, for like millions of war-torn people, I comforted myself with the old cliché 'It will never happen to me'. Twice bombs dropped close and twice I ran to my mother who, in no uncertain terms, sent me back to my bed. Both boys slept soundly; John snored loudly, and little Billy's bright blue eyes were tightly closed. Suddenly the cacophony outside reached top C with a third piercing whine.

Naked terror gripped. I slipped my legs floorwards, as a violent force hurled me backwards and downwards, inexorably pulling while bricks and mortar fell incessantly. Instinct said 'fight!' and I fought. I wriggled, I pulled, I tugged, oblivious of pain, knowing innately that this was a life-and-death battle, and all the time the masonry continued to obey the force of gravity, raining over me like confetti. 'Oh God!' I prayed, 'Get me out of here.' Suddenly that frightening, unseen vortex, so virulent and compelling, ceased, and I was thrown like a rag-doll onto the remains of my bed. I was free. Billy's terrified screams rent the air.

Activity took over – respite was denied me. Mother's practicality overrode her anxiety. Poor John, always a nervous child, after a horrendous awakening was told to take me to the shelter. I was bred in a society that accepted raw life and recognised authority as sacrosanct, and although weak and traumatised, I followed meekly. The room was filled with dense dust and, choking and spluttering, clinging to one another, we emerged into the inferno that was the night.

Reaching comparative safety, shaking, I sat on a bunk. John lit a candle; he took one look at my quaking body. 'Mary! You're covered in blood.' Seeing the utter horror on my beloved young brother's face, I tried to assure him that I was fine, as the wardens burst in and an ambulance shrieked to a standstill. The noise was as deafening as ever, and now fine rain was falling and the shrapnel sizzled as it fell. I was placed on a stretcher on the pavement, while the ambulance was being reorganised to make room for my mother, who had reappeared. I lay prone and vulnerable, petrified that one of the red-hot pieces of metal would land on a vital area of my quivering body.

In the darkened hospital ward, two ghostly figures came to my bed and put many stitches in a large head wound. All the while the devil's orchestra played on outside, and my neighbour patients moved restlessly in their beds. The night wore on, and at about 4 a.m. the beautiful sound of the all-clear pierced the air, as sleep, welcome sleep, descended.

Meanwhile Billy was carried, screaming, first by my mother and then by a passing soldier, and taken to the first aid post on a nearby hill. After assessment he joined me at Surbiton Hospital. Billy's face was a mask of embedded minute pieces of mortar and brick, most of which the doctors pulled out by hand. Incredibly his face healed well, without a single scar.

I sustained several large abrasions, and largish lumps of lath, plaster and bricks were removed from my body. We were both kept in hospital until our wounds healed. Once home, in spite of the nightly raids, life resumed normality. From a platform of 68 years I look back and marvel at the ability of the ordinary people to deal with death-dealing situations as cheerfully and efficiently as possible, and then resume life at peacetime pace as if nothing had happened.

At first it was thought that a shell had exploded and was responsible for the crater behind my bed, but during a later inspection an unexploded bomb was discovered. Panic stations ensued, and everyone was evacuated. The army bomb demolition squad removed the 500-pound bomb and presented my father with the mangled remains of a fin, where, in a crumpled crevice, a light cluster of small feathers from my pillow were to be seen.

John meanwhile had suffered a severe shock and spent a week in bed with a high temperature. In those days counselling was unheard of, and shock from traumatic events was an everyday occurrence. It was the duty of us all to survive, to rely on those pragmatic, innermost strengths of humour and common sense. But the balance of the brain is fragile and poor John was unable to cope. In a very short time it became obvious that he was mentally disturbed, although he held an important clerical position in a local factory for two or three years until he was eventually diagnosed as schizophrenic.

We never returned to the cottage, and our next home was on the outskirts of Ewell. We were all pretty traumatised; at least 20 houses in the immediate vicinity were demolished, with some loss of life. We slept on two large mattresses on the dining-room floor – a wise move, as loving human contact was vital. Mother and I were at one end, and it was comforting to cuddle her when the noise reached a crescendo as a bomb dropped too close.

After the war Bill joined the Navy, got married and had three children. He lived a stone's throw from our parents and was a great comfort to my mother, who suffered from Alzheimer's for the last 15 years of her life. Father lived to be 80, and Bill died not long after Dad from a brain tumour, which devastated his young family. John spent the last 50 years of his life in a mental home; I lost him in 1995, aged 69.

This was the tragic saga of my beloved family. I viewed most of these events from afar, as I served three years in the WAAF, married another John, a Welshman, and settled in the Conwy Valley in North Wales where we too brought up three children.

Quite recently a family matter determined a visit south and on a whim I decided to visit my old home. The footpath fronting the row of cottages was sunny, and I noticed that the very large elms that once overhung the path were mere stumps, having succumbed to Dutch Elm Disease. I reached our old gate and hung over it, just as I did 60-plus years ago.

A few Busy Lizzies poked their heads up instead of the pansies that were once so popular, and the front door was of modern design. Number 6 appeared deserted, and I didn't knock. I just wanted to soak up the atmosphere; everywhere there were memories of my happy childhood. Soft music lilted from next door, and my eyes darted to the roof. But the smooth slates were uniform; no sign of the carnage that had taken place that war-torn night. As my mind drifted I watched John and Billy playing hopscotch whilst my beautiful mother shelled peas on the front doorstep.

How many millions of Jews and displaced persons can recall similar harmonious scenes of an idyllic childhood? They all suffered so much more than I, and yet the pain that was seeded that horrendous evening in September 1940 haunts me still.

6

Food during the Second World War

I was just 15 when food was first rationed in the Second World War. At first the portions of butter, cheese, margarine, bacon, meat, sugar and tea were quite generous, but as the war progressed and food from abroad dried up due to the success of the German U-Boat campaign, rations became smaller and smaller and meals scantier. Some foods were never rationed, namely most fish, vegetables and fruit, although if my memory is correct, potatoes were rationed for a short period, as was bread. A points scheme was introduced as luxury foods became scarce, and this ascertained a certain fairness of distribution for goods such as tinned meat, commercial jam, tinned fish and dried fruits, which were all only available occasionally.

Everyone was issued with a ration book, and each household was required to register with a butcher and grocer who would tear a coupon from the ration book every time an itemed portion was bought. Unrationed food was subject to availability; the grapevine was in fine fettle, and word would go around that cod could be obtained from Bloggs the fishmongers in the morning, and by nine o'clock the resultant queue would be a mile long even after a heavy night of bombing. Some items such as lemons and bananas, so prolific on stalls and in the greengrocer shops before the war, disappeared overnight. Onions, too, were unobtainable unless you were fortunate enough to have an allotment or large garden. The government urged everyone to 'Dig for Victory', but this wasn't always practical, for in my suburb most people travelled a 30-mile return journey to the city of London daily despite nightly air raids, plus regular duties as air raid wardens, part-time soldiers and fire watchers.

When rationing started in 1940 it was made clear that restaurants would remain open for service, although at first the populace grumbled at the unfairness, thinking that as usual the ordinary folk would miss out, but the system worked well. The eating houses were allocated food on a strict rationing basis, and generally non-rationed foods were the norm, with beans on toast one of the favourites. If, however, meat was served the portions were only a fraction of the size of today's helpings. Of course, first-class establishments like the Ritz may have been and probably were allocated better-class food-stuffs and larger amounts.

Towards the end of the war the government saw the need for good reasonable dining places and launched the British Restaurant scheme throughout England and Wales. These were chiefly manned by volunteers and were mainly held in local halls. The meals were well cooked and wholesome, and the restaurants were patronised by everyone. Also I think I am right in stating that they continued for several years after the war.

Before America entered the war, we were favoured with the lend-lease scheme, and Spam, dried egg and powdered milk appeared on grocers' shelves. Before long mothers and restaurants alike were making dried-egg omelettes. I hated them, and couldn't believe they were hens' eggs dried, the taste was so alien.

In 1942 I joined the Women's Auxiliary Air Force and became an aircraft engine mechanic. The food at the camps and airfields varied; at one the piles of plates at the serving hatch in the cookhouse regularly housed cockroaches. At another, the cook's speciality was roast potatoes that were served daily. Unfortunately, they were case hardened, and a friend broke a tooth on one. The peas were like bullets and the gravy thin and tasteless. A duty officer regularly toured the cookhouse at mealtimes, but no one ever complained. I think my generation accepted life as it was, and made the best of it. We were too thankful that we weren't under the heel of Hitler.

I spent my longest spell of service at Rednal in Shropshire, where the food was reasonably good, but an awful lot found its way into the pig bin, which was disturbing, for each service person was allocated a double civilian ration as well as the best of the rationed food.

It was at Rednal that I met John, who was to be my husband of almost 60 years. Before he left Britain for a spell of foreign service, I spent a few days with him and his family at their house at Hendre near Conwy, which has been my home for the last 30 years.

Whilst John was abroad I spent several leaves with his parents and gained an insight into the local food chain. All the farms came under the jurisdiction of the War Agricultural Executive Committee, known locally as the 'War Ag,' who employed experienced farm labourers to work with and guide the local farmers. They were also responsible for the Italian prisoners who worked on the land thereabouts. These prisoners were housed at a camp above the river at Tyn y Groes. Each farm was under strict instruction; a certain amount of farmland had to be arable, and only a small percentage of produce could be retained by the farmer for his own use. This included eggs, and a friend of mine who lived on a farm as a small child remembers receiving half an egg for breakfast when the hens were broody. Many farms also employed land girls.

In the main, however, the rural community fared better food-wise than their town counterparts. Cottagers were allowed to keep a few hens and, I believe, even a pig, although not many had the facilities for an animal. All kept large vegetable gardens, for they weren't hounded by air raids like the town dwellers, and with fewer civic duties, had more time.

No account of wartime food would be complete without a mention of fish, which was never rationed but was subject to erratic availability in the towns, where the fish and chip shops opened only at weekends and, in many cases, disappeared altogether. Here in Conwy, with fish on the Quay, the situation was better, although I have been told that a certain percentage had to be sent away.

In those dark days women needed a vivid imagination and much ingenuity to make scanty ingredients palatable. One day my mother appeared with a pile of potatoes, a turnip, a parsnip and three carrots, and threw them on the table with disgust, uttering the despairing, 'How on earth can I make a meal with these?' Eventually the two of us concocted a very palatable meal. We boiled all the veg with salt, mashed the potatoes, and placed them around the edge of a large meat plate. Inside we packed the rest and garnished them with thick Oxo gravy flavoured with a pinch of herbs. For five hungry people it was a good meal. Innovation was the order of the day, and potato was used in many guises – pastry and bread being but two.

A Lancastrian friend of mine who was fortunate enough to possess a very new gadget – a pressure cooker – begged bones from the butcher, pressure-cooked them until they were chalk, used the liquid for soup, and the gleaned fat to make pastry and, luxury of luxuries, homemade chips.

The sugar ration was extremely small and many women drank tea sugarless, saving the precious commodity for other purposes. Sometime mid-war, an allocation of sugar for jam-making became available. Families collected berries from the hedgerows and bought cheap fruit. Also, obscure recipes such as marrow and ginger jam were dug out from old recipe books and proved sure winners. About this time the authorities approached the Women's Institute (WI) with a proposition to collect fruit and make jam in field kitchens. In 1976 a lady from Llandudno Junctiion WI gave a talk on this subject. She, as a young woman, had taken part in this project. Later in 1998 when Conwy WI moved its headquarters from the Guildhall to the Church House, a very large preserving pan was unearthed, suggesting that Conwy too had been engaged in making large amounts of jam.

During the war I had three memorable meals. The first occurred early in 1943 when I was a trainee flight mechanic at Hednesford in Staffordshire, and a friend promised me a special birthday treat. After a very long walk on Cannock Chase we ended up in an obscure farmhouse in a breathtaking valley where the farmer's wife served mouth-watering eggs and bacon – what ambrosia! At that time I hadn't tasted a real egg for at least two years.

D-Day took place on 6th June 1944, and all leave was cancelled. It was reinstated in October, and I arranged to spend mine with my mother and aunt at my grandmother's house in Cheltenham. My welcoming meal was fabulous; they had scrimped and saved to make it special, and the first course was preserved pears, which I loved. As we ate we chatted about the family and, suddenly realising that nothing had been said about my eldest brother, who had been suffering from nerves due to the buzz bombs and V-2s, I asked how he was. My mother went quiet, then gently broke the news that he had been diagnosed as a schizophrenic. For years after that pears were missing from my diet. That was one of the saddest days of my life.

The third meal was my wedding breakfast at Veale's Restaurant – above the shop on Castle Street, Conwy, a fixture for nigh on 60 years – on 29th November 1945. John had returned from abroad three months earlier and, like many other couples at that time, we took the plunge and tied the knot. Mrs Veale did us proud, but the one-tier wedding cake was the *pièce de résistance*, for my mother-in-law had sacrificed her precious food points to purchase the sugar and dried fruit.

It was the lot of the women of the nation, as in all modern wars, to squeeze blood from stones, to create an era of people judged by later statistics to be the fittest and skinniest generation of the last half-century.

7

Aftermath

After the bomb came the aftermath, quite the worst time of my life. Having always been of a nervous disposition, I found cycling home after work along a dark road with sirens wailing wasn't the best method of recuperation. I was terrified. Luckily I worked with my brother John, so I was not alone when shrapnel hissed and bombs fell nearby. My employment at that time was as a cost clerk at a factory that produced light engineering and sparking plugs for all types of combustion engines, situated at the Putney end of the A3 road, about 7 miles from my new home at Worcester Park.

Our new home lay amidst a welter of semi-detached houses where the residents were the typical reserved southerners of that time, living self-contained, quiet lives and having little contact with anyone, only their own kith and kin. Having come from a village atmosphere in Surbiton, that was teeming with old school friends, evening activities and nosey neighbours, I found myself extremely lonely and raided the rather small local library. I read copiously, augmenting my rather limited education with any book, from Rider Haggard to Charles Darwin.

Once Hitler realised that the spirit of the English people was not easily broken, he turned his attentions to Russia and started another brutal wartime front. The air raids became sporadic and life much more peaceful, but intensely boring for an impression-able teenager who missed her old friends.

In September 1942, having reached the age of eighteen, I decided to join the WAAF, not with any patriotic notions, but because like all teenagers I craved the society of youngsters of my own age. So one lunchtime I attended the recruiting office in Kingston, only to be told, 'Come back when you're eighteen.' This particular problem had harassed me for some time, having been regularly offered a half-fare bus ticket available only to under 14-year-olds. Heavens above! What effrontery to a mature lady of 18. Determined to end my lonely existence, and eager for any adventure, I returned that evening armed with my father and my birth certificate. Bliss! Oh heavenly bliss, I was accepted. Goodbye, stultifying dreary life, welcome, come what may!

Unfortunately the parting with my family hurt more than I had anticipated. Mum watched dutifully as I walked that early morning along our crescent on my way to the bus stop, en route to my new life. She told me years later that she knew that day I had left the nest for good, and her tears flowed, for our family life together had been very happy and I was the first of her chicks to fly.

On arriving at the recruiting office, I was taken with 20 other recruits to the sorting depot at Gloucester, where we stayed for only one week. Here we were stripped of our rather motley indi-viduality and dressed like all other WAAFs in the standard Air Force blue. Morecambe in Lancashire was our next destination, where we suffered three weeks of marching, blisters, injections, lectures and an initiation into a totally new life. My billet was a second-class holiday boarding house where the landlady coped single-handedly (for her husband was a squaddy abroad) with four children and eight WAAFs. We were fed adequately but boringly in not-too-clean surroundings, where we thrived and emerged at the end of the training period fortified by enough basic knowledge and stamina to see us through this very traumatic time of our young lives.

I had been designated as a balloon operator at Gloucester and after leaving Morecambe was sent to a balloon training base at Kidbrooke in south-east London. I lapped up the experience and soon became 'teacher's pet'. At that time barrage balloons surrounded all our major cities, and of course London had the most. The course was quite intensive and was a mishmash of theory and manual handling.

The end of the course heralded three weeks manning a sited balloon whilst still training for the final exam. Two WAAF NCOs were in charge and we all lived in a nearby hut. Two instructors attended daily.

Towards the end of the course a very dramatic but natural occurrence shattered our hitherto quiet lives, for the German air raids had practically ceased at that stage in the war. That particular day had been pretty breezy, but the wind was not really belligerent until the evening, when the two WAAF guards burst into the billet and yelled that the balloon was out of control and a gale was imminent. Our sergeant immediately ordered everyone outside to their stations, ready to haul the balloon down. The balloon was anchored by a large cable fastened to 3-foot solid concrete blocks, and the whole unit stood on a base of concrete. During the course we had been consistently warned of the danger of causing a spark by banging the blocks onto the base, as the balloon was filled with inflammable hydrogen.

The winch operator started to lower this huge, dangerous, inflated monster, but the wind had other ideas, its speed increasing every second. On the ground, with every cable and block manned by a WAAF, we waited, seeing nothing as lights were forbidden. Britain maintained a strict black-out policy throughout the war.

Suddenly the balloon was on the ground. The sergeant screamed, 'Get its nose to wind', but this monstrous creature was alive, the cables were alive, and the whole site was a frightening scene. We struggled for control but were powerless, just paper dolls, buffeted by this mad, bad, cruel force that has killed many a sailor battling high on the mast of a sailing ship.

Driving rain now entered the scene, and we were soon drenched. The blocks danced in our hands, and we were powerless to stop them striking the ground. An explosion seemed imminent; naked terror gripped us all. Then at the very moment that the potent power was at its most dangerous it became our saviour, for suddenly and without warning the balloon rent from nose to stern and its dangerous contents blew harmlessly away to the four corners of the earth.

Dejected and feeling very guilty, every one of us nursing damaged limbs, we returned to the hut. We were very unsure as to our fate, for the hierarchy of the RAF frowned upon failure, however extenuating the circumstances.

Luckily more momentous news greeted us next day, and our minutes of madness and terror were buried forever. The government had decided that a barrage of balloons was no longer needed to encircle our large cities. Everyone was to be remustered, our course was obsolete, and all the 'gen' we had dutifully imbibed over the last months was wasted. But then, is knowledge ever wasted?

My next port of call was No. 6 of TT (Technical Training), for I was now to become a flight mechanic and learn all about aircraft engines – and at that time I hadn't the faintest idea what a piston was. As before, I lapped up the theory – I was always happy to learn – but the practical side was another matter. Whilst my friends had no trouble assembling engine parts and making metal articles, I was hopeless. I still am at anything that requires manual handling. At the final exam, which was mainly theoretical, I topped the list, but my hand-made spanner resembled a piece of the shrapnel my brother Billy so ardently collected when the air raids were persistent.

My new home after passing the exam was to be in Shropshire

and was to be my main residence for the next two years; 61OTU (Officers Training Unit) situated at Rednal, a hamlet nine miles from Oswestry, was a finishing school for pilots assigned to Spitfires. I was now a qualified flight mechanic with the rank of Aircraft Woman 2nd Class, the lowest rank in the WAAF, and I think, if my memory is correct, that my pay was £1 a fortnight. But as you progressed up the rankings your pay increased, and two years later when a corporal the princely sum of £4 every two weeks was my lot.

The airfield possessed three runways set in a triangle (wind dictated which one would be used), the perimeter track encircled the runways and was the main road, and the four flights A, B, C and D were placed at strategic points on this airfield highway. Each student pilot was allocated to one of these out stations where they were required to perform a certain number of flying hours before being let loose on the enemy.

X Squadron, where gunnery and other specialist subjects were taught, was at the far corner of the airfield, and for my sins was my workplace. My best friend Helen MacIntosh (Mac) was on D flight.

One fine June day in 1943, Mac and I had managed to get a day off together – no mean feat – and were waiting on the tiny station platform at the Rednal railway halt, en route for Shrewsbury, when a fellow RAF chap arrived. I coloured immediately, because he had been the subject of a conversation I had had with a colleague.

'Who's that tall boy?!' I'd asked my friend. 'Oh,' she replied, 'he's too old for you, he's 27', and as an afterthought, 'He's got false teeth and he's married.' How my husband and I laughed over this statement in years to come, for he was barely 21 and he certainly wasn't married. The only tiny scrap of conversation that was correct was the false teeth accusation.

The upshot of this meeting culminated in a very happy and joyous day together in Shrewsbury, including a trip on the river for the three of us, during which time Mac and I learned that he was indeed only 21, his name was John Richard Williams, and his hometown was Conwy, North Wales.

The hour-long river trip was particularly enjoyable for there was much good-humoured banter until we disembarked, and the boat man, with a large grin, held up the business end of a small suspender (a contraption used before the advent of tights to keep a woman's stockings up). The crowd who were waiting for the boats laughed. I coloured and Mac emphatically denied any involvement. John roared, and I loved him from that moment. Ooh la la! Ain't love grand? On examination back at the billet, the despised article was found to belong to neither of us and had probably been in the bottom of the boat for ages.

After only three short months of spending every possible waking moment together, John was posted abroad and was on the first convoy through the Mediterranean Sea and the Suez Canal since Dunkirk. It was a horrific time for him; the ship was torpedoed and everyone lucky enough to survive was transferred to another boat which, horror of horrors, had leaky water tanks. Salt water seeped in and the airmen became ill. When the boat finally docked at Capetown only John and another lad were able to walk off – the rest were stretchered or carried.

Unfortunately for my beloved, his nightmare was not over, for within a fortnight of landing he contracted diphtheria and was put on the danger list. The telegram to his mother frightened us all, but in a few days another arrived declaring John over the worst. Unfortunately, the disease left a heart murmur, but he recovered and led a very healthy life for 60 years until cancer ravaged his system and he died aged 82 in 2004.

There is one small hugely funny but very poignant incident that took place on that isolation ward in faraway South Africa. John, denied any ordinary contact with other people, for he was in a ward on his own, was bored to death once he began to recuperate. He was no reader, not like me who devoured books like a hungry wolf, so he devised a method of amusement. Annoyed by the dozens of flies that buzzed incessantly, when one alighted on the hygienically clean white wall, with the aid of his finger and a bottle of disinfectant, he ringed each one and watched the poor fly struggle to get away.

When the doctor arrived he shook with laughter, but looked with horror at John and said, 'We must do something about you', and promptly took him off the contagious list.

The British government had an agreement with Jan Smuts, the Premier, to use South African facilities to train our pilots. At that time there was a very strong anti-British, anti-coloured underground movement in South Africa that was to surface and take power after the war. Churchill and his minions were aware of this, and every airman sent to this apparently idyllic country undertook a period of intense military training before leaving the UK. As it happened, no large incident occurred whilst John was out there, but he was incensed by the existing inhuman attitude to the coloured population, never realising that the Smuts regime was mild compared to what was to come after the war.

Life on an airfield back in Shropshire continued on an uneventful note; intake after intake of pilots arrived, were processed and packed off, presumably wiser and more proficient. Just after John left, a film unit arrived with a Wellington bomber, several Gloucester Gladiator fighter planes and a Gipsy Moth. They were tucked away in a corner of the airfield and became Q flight.

I was one of the ground staff allocated from our main station but the pilots were specialists and came from elsewhere. *Signed with their Honour* was the name of the film-to-be. The cameraman was a famous chap called Osmond Borradaile, and Alexander Korda was either the producer or director, I can't remember which. All this sounds most alluring, but to us ordinary airmen and airwomen, it was just a job of work.

Whilst John was in South Africa we got engaged, and we married after the war. On his first leave after his return he introduced me to his beloved Conwy, a historic North Wales castle town on the coast. Always full of laughter and ready to tease, he took me on a tour of the old town with the hope that I would put my foot on a mythical stone, that was supposed to ensure the permanent return of anyone fortunate or unfortunate enough to encounter it. I found it, for 65 years later, I'm still here!

8

Out of the Frying Pan, into the Fire

There is no doubt about it: that year was the most unusual, the most interesting, as well as being the most historic of my entire 85 years. The year, of course, was 1945; it was also the turning point in millions of people's lives when horror receded and a fresh life beckoned. It was also the occasion of my twenty-first birthday, my fiancé John's return from abroad, my wedding, my demob from the WAAF, and the start of my first pregnancy.

So much has been written about the end of that dreadful time that swallowed almost all my teenage years, about the euphoria and the exultation at being freed from Hitler's long arm. At Rednal, where I was stationed at the time, we celebrated quietly. The camp had two recreational halls; one was the NAAFI where lotto (bingo) was held regularly and there was a snooker table and darts board. The staff were most welcoming and tea and small cakes were always available, but for me the atmosphere was cold. After John's departure in 1943, I rarely went there, preferring the alternative venue, the YMCA hall, which was run by a very small staff augmented by local volunteers. One of these ladies, the owner of a local mansion with an immense garden, arrived with armfuls of spring shrubs with which we decorated the hall.

Together with my friends I spent a very happy contemplative day, thankful that at last it was all over. Luckily, perhaps, I could not foresee the near future, for an uncomfortable time lay ahead.

51

John arrived back in the UK in August and we got married in November. It was a quiet ceremony held in the old local church where John's ancestors had worshipped for centuries. Being an airwoman I was not entitled to any coupons, but my sister-in-law gave me a very nice, slightly worn suit. The up-to-date hat (no coupons) was purchased in Epsom, where my parents lived, plus my high-heeled shoes for which Mum donated the coupons.

Those shoes turned out to be a blessing in disguise for I possessed, but didn't realise it, slightly dislocated ankles which gave way every few steps. The pain was so bad that I stuck them for the wedding and then discarded them for evermore, being thoroughly happy for the rest of my life with the flatties I had worn throughout my service career. Consequently, at 85 I have near perfect feet – no corns or bunions and nary a visit to a chiropodist.

Our reception was held in a local baker's. Mother-in-law supplied the coupons for the fruit for the cake. By today's standards everything was very frugal, but to me it was a banquet straight from heaven, used as I was to good food badly cooked in mess halls.

After a short leave we spent three honeymoon days in Betws-y-Coed, then returned to our respective camps. Mine at that time was in Wiltshire, 61OTU having moved lock, stock and barrel some time during the preceding summer.

I was demobbed in December, exactly a fortnight after my returning to work. We managed to get rooms in Beverley in Yorkshire and John travelled daily to his base in Leconfield around 9 miles away. The weather during the early part of 1946 was dour, stark and damp, and I hated East Yorkshire. I missed the easy camaraderie of my fellow airwomen, and John worked late at the airfield so I hardly saw him.

By this time it became obvious and was corroborated medically that I was to produce an offspring in early autumn. So it was deemed wise for me to return to John's home in Hendre, Conwy. As Tyddyn

Melus was extremely small in those days, I obtained two rooms in Bryn Goleu, a neighbour's house. Water was drawn from a well, but electricity had been installed just before the war.

I was over the moon to leave the northeast: a more dour place I had yet to come across, but no doubt the inhabitants adore it just as I do North Wales – is there a more enchanted place? Unfortunately, it was not all roses in Conwy at that time. I still found time hung heavily, and I still missed the airmen and women. In October my first child, Gwena, was born, and I found life a nightmare. Young and inexperienced and used to the amenities of a suburban life, cooking on an open sitting-room fire plus carrying water became a daily hazard, and in those days I wasn't a tidy person. The pans coated with fire soot managed to deposit black dirt everywhere.

John, who was demobbed just before Gwena arrived in 1946, had returned to his peacetime job as a mechanic in a garage in nearby Colwyn Bay. Cars were much dirtier in those days. He fondled the baby continually and even when his hands were clean, oil seemed to exude from them. He smeared the cot blankets and the baby, who no doubt benefited as, after the first few months when she cried continually, she was a sunny child.

It was a hectic time, mucky and messy, and when the big freeze came in January 1947 life became a matter of survival. Electric cuts were regular events and coal, already stringently rationed, became increasingly difficult to obtain. The house was always cold, and my landlady, who was over 80, was not in good health.

Gwena was still in her screaming period, not being six months until the April. One day, the temperature registering freezing, we ran out of water. John always made sure we had plenty before he went to work, but washing had emptied the crock, and by 4 p.m. the baby was screaming for a bottle and old Mrs Jones longed for a cup of tea.

The well was situated at the bottom of a flight of steps, and the pump that serviced it had long since been cast aside, being completely useless in frozen conditions. The well was deep and to obtain water one needed to throw the bucket, which was attached to a rope, so that it landed sideways on the surface of the water. The bucket would fill and be drawn up quickly by means of the rope. I found this operation impossible; the bucket would not sink and fill, but floated harmlessly on the surface of the water. After half an hour, and almost frozen solid, I managed to half-fill the bucket. Triumphant, I carried my trophy carefully up the icy steps only to slip on the top one and lose my precious water. The baby screamed until John came home two hours later, and Mrs Jones and I went tea-less.

With spring things got a little better and we managed to rent an unsanitary cottage at Groesffordd, half a mile up Hendre Road, where we lived until we successfully managed to obtain a council house eight years later. The rented house was tiny, and again water was obtained 300 yards away from a pump. This pump was more satisfactory and, in all the years I used it, gave of its bounty freely and without hindrance. The whole house was damp, but it had a roof and we were happy there. Hugh my elder son arrived in March 1949 and Richard was born in 1953.

One laughable incident occurred when we lived in the Groesffordd cottage. Hugh was about 14 months and still in nappies when the weather turned arid and hot, and stayed that way for months. My neighbours and I normally collected rainwater for washing, but rain was a no-hope that summer. Fed up with carrying water up a steep hill, my friend Phil and I came up with a novel idea. We balanced a large 6-foot bath on Hugh's pram and filled it with water, a somewhat precarious procedure as the bath was very unstable. However, we eventually succeeded and carefully guided the top-heavy pram onto the road. At that very moment the local bus appeared, and in our hurry to move out of the way, the bath turned turtle and drowned me in our precious water. The whole bus was in an uproar; we unfortunately were not. It was back to carrying buckets, no more adventures with prams and baths.

When we were living with Mrs Jones at Bryn Goleu, we tried for a council house in Conwy. Our fellow service returnees were receiving them as a matter of course. We were turned down because we lived outside Conwy in the rural area where no council houses were being built. This, in spite of the fact that we had nine years' war service between us.

Finally, after living for eight years in the very unhealthy Groesffordd cottage, Nant Conwy Rural Council built 12 council houses in an adjoining field. They were allocated to one couple not yet married, three more who lived out of the area, and another pair who had been married six weeks. We were not on the list. I cried. My darling husband laughed and said he was enjoying the struggle.

Well, we fought. That evening we attended our MP's surgery and he told us to make the biggest fuss, write to everybody including the local paper, get up a petition, and ask all our neighbours and friends to do the same. We did all of these things and we were finally allocated Number 7, due to the original intended tenant's withdrawal. I was over the moon; regular baths for us all. Water, water everywhere. Only people denied regular sanitation know that real luxury is a hot bath, whenever they require it.

We had written to the Queen, the Prime Minister, the Welsh Office, the papers, we organised a petition, we berated the councillors for allocating houses to newly-weds when ex-service personnel had waited eight years for a decent house. Did the councillors get their knuckles rapped from the powers that be? That I didn't know or didn't care. I had a decent house for my kids and husband, and that was all I cared about!

We lived happily in that house for 22 years, rearing three children and numerous cats and dogs. We moved in 1975 when we extended Tyddyn Melus.

9

Hendre Fawr

During the 1950s a distant cousin of John's spent some time unearthing our family history, many moons before the current hot trend for awareness of one's forebears, when there was no Internet for easy reference.

Somehow or other he came up with the knowledge that Archbishop John Williams and Oliver Cromwell were ancestors of our line of Williamses. Being sceptical, I made for the local church museum and unearthed a parish register from 1700 onwards. Apparently this would not be possible today, as all old parish registers are housed at Aberystwyth University.

The earliest reference to our Williams was in 1709, 'Johannes Williams de Hendre'. The whole register was written in higgledy-piggledy Latin script with scarcely any plain paper to be seen.

After Johannes it was impossible to decipher anything until the end of the century when Humphrey and Grace came along, but I was no nearer finding out if our Williamses were descended from Cromwell. I abandoned the chase, and to this day we do not know whether our family are descendants of the direct line.

Humphrey and Grace's heir was William Williams, John's great-grandfather, who was quite an accomplished man. He was the parish clerk at the local church of St Benedict's and, as such, was required to read and write, sing and lead the choir. He was the ancestor who bought Tyddyn Melus in 1869 with the intention of retiring there, but unfortunately he died that year, and his widow decided to continue farming the main holding with hired help plus the assistance of her eldest son John, who moved into Tyddyn Melus with his wife Ellen and young family.

John had three sons and one daughter. The eldest, Richard, farmed Hendre Fawr after his father's death. He never married and his sister Margaret (Maggie) kept house for him. William married late and was the farmer bailiff at the Oakwood Hotel for many years. The youngest son, John, married Anne Jane of Hendre Bach, and their eldest son, Hugh John, became my father-in-law.

John's wife Ellen was, like all farm women, hardworking and dedicated. She was from a small valley nearer the River Conwy in a house where several of her siblings died of one of the virulent contagious diseases prevalent at that time. Her parents were distraught, and her father swore the house was to blame and moved the family to another farm, Bwlch Mawr, in what he considered a more healthy environment. He then proceeded to set fire to the old property, and razed it to the ground.

Sometime in the late 1960s I was walking in that vicinity with Hughie John when he espied a large bay tree and declared this the site of his grandmother's first ill-fated home. He was much moved.

The old Williams family were held in high regard by all the local people as I was to find out in 1947. I desperately required a new saucepan – mine had a large hole and the handle was very unstable. At that time obtaining a replacement was practically impossible, but someone suggested that Miss Jones (Tinman) might be able to help. This single lady kept a queer shop in Conwy; there was nothing in the window, but apparently she had supplied many scarce articles during the war. I entered the rather dank dark shop with a little trepidation, and a very old lady emerged from behind the counter. I was lucky: she said she had a good pan for sale, and produced a

Top: Merryman Organ, walking the greyhounds, 1890

Right:
My Granny, a Jekyll and Hyde character, 1910

Top: My father-in-law carting coal for Hendre Bach, 1915

Right: Gran's Wonder Babe - 'Me', 1924

Top: My brother John, prior to heartbreak, 1937

Right: Sally (Roberts) Williams with John in 1943

Top: Working on a Gladiator with a colleague on Film Flight, 1943

Right: A copy of this photo of me was kept in John's tunic pocket throughout his period abroad (hence the fold), 1943

Right: My wedding day, November 1945

Bottom: Mrs. Beatrice (Reynolds) Jones, Peter's grandmother, about 1956 (See Chapter 'Rapport')

Top: Poised for action, Cymro 1974

Right: A builder's apprentice? John, 1975, renovating the cottage

Top: Tyddyn Melus, Welsh for Sweet Cottage

Right: My grandchildren baby Dewi, Robert and my daughter Gwena and I, feeding a lamb, 1980

Top: Prince Charles showing complete interest chatting to me, 2004

Bottom: Springtime, my sons Hugh and Richard with our present dog Spot, 2009

solid second-hand saucepan from under the counter. I was overjoyed, and paid for it as we got talking.

She asked me if I was living locally; I explained who I was, and she started telling me about John's great-uncle Richard and his brothers. 'They were very upright people and always ready to help anyone in trouble.' She added with emphasis, 'They were gentlemen.'

I also learned another piece of rural history from that old lady's lips. In Victorian times there was no sanitation as we know it. Human waste was deposited in chamber pots and bins hidden under cunningly formed seats. Well, apparently all excreta in country areas was used on the fields in the same way as cattle and horse manure is used today.

Victorian John died before the First World War and his grandson married Sally in 1915. When Maggie died they went to live at Hendre Fawr, for Sally to take charge of the house. Hugh at that time was employed as a gardener, and he preferred that work to helping on the farm.

In 1922 John was born and Betty in 1925. In 1927 Great-Uncle Richard decided to retire. The slump was affecting farm prices in a way never seen before. The work was long and arduous, and he was 64 years old. He asked Hugh John to take on the farm, but John's father thought that with the precarious situation possibly lasting a few more years, he deemed it expedient to keep his job.

So the whole family moved after the farm was sold to what is now my beloved cottage. On the day of the auction, Sally realised that the two china dogs she had planned to take with her to the cottage had lot numbers on them and were on the auctioneer's list. Rather than make a fuss she decided to bid for them, but got called to the kitchen when the hammer was about to fall. A local lady bought them, but when Sally approached her afterwards, explained the situation, and asked if she could buy the dogs, she met with a blank refusal. And there the matter rested for 30 years or more.

Sometime in the early 1960s, John was driving home quite late when he met an old friend on the road. 'Do you want a lift, Hugh?' he called, and the man jumped in. He was a neighbour who lived in the cottages at Hendre.

On alighting, Hugh said, 'Wait a minute, John. I have something for you.' He came back with a large newspaper parcel which he handed to John. He said, 'My mother bought these dogs from the Hendre Fawr auction back in 1927. Your mother wanted to buy them back but was turned down. I want you to have them because your Uncle Richard was kind to me, and I had a happy time in Hendre Fawr. He also bought me my first pair of long trousers.'

The dogs have remained on my dresser ever since, in pride of place.

10

Victorian Hendre Bach

The soft tone of a saw could be heard as one approached this Conwy Valley farm on a late November afternoon in 1875, when daylight had gone and the wind blew icicles from the north-east. As one approached the house a large pit could be seen; in the pit was the small, slight wife of the house and in her hand was one end of a large cross-cut saw. Sawing above her was her husband, the farmer, and they worked together, sawing plank after plank to make a consignment of coffins. Also in the pit was their youngest working child, and he held aloft a candle.

The farmer farmed 30 acres at Hendre Bach, just a mile from Conwy. He was Joseph Jones, born in Rowen in 1844. Orphaned at a young age, he was adopted by a family believed to be relatives, who also lived in Rowen at a farm called Isallt. Little is known of his early days, but during some horseplay with other youngsters he lost the tip of a little finger. In about 1870 he married Anne Jane Jones, from Llandudno, and was able financially to take the tenancy of Hendre Bach and stock it, no mean task for an orphan in those days. Both Joseph and his wife were small and slight, yet they raised ten children – five boys and five girls.

Joseph was a very remarkable man, for he not only ran a 30-acre farm which in later years, by renting land, he increased to 68 acres. He was also a wheelwright, and operated an early threshing machine.

His other ventures included a transport business, carrying coal and hay to outlying farms, and making and delivering coffins and farm furniture, for he was an accomplished carpenter. Another lucrative employment was the building of local houses and walls; some houses he built for others on a contract basis and some he built for himself and sold for profit. Gypsy Glen was one of these and was built about 1885. It still stands four-square on the Henryd Road, just above Hendre.

Eventually Joseph bought Hendre Bach outright, but in the early days the farm was rented and the owner lived in Abergele. Once a fortnight Anne Jane walked the 12 miles to Abergele with the rent money sewn into the hem of her skirt. Apparently this was necessary because pickpockets abounded on the coast road. This meant a 24-mile round trip for an already busy farm mother, and more often than not she was pregnant with a child.

As soon as the children were old enough they became employees. Joseph taught four of the five boys the trade of carpentry. As far as is known, all the children were involved in the working of the farm except two of the girls who went into service. Until 1900 or there-abouts, there appears to have been no settled school in the district, so the local children were put to work at an early age. The Hendre Bach youngsters were no exception and were expected to tackle any task allotted to them. The youngest working child's task was to hold the candle in the saw pit so that his or her elders could continue to do outside work long after sundown.

Anne Jane was a determined little lady with an acid-drop for a tongue; not afraid of hard work, she, like millions of Victorian women, tackled the formidable challenges of her lifetime with forti-tude and courage. Arising about 5 a.m. she lit a fire (no electricity or firelighters), put a kettle on to boil for a quick cuppa, and helped the men with the milking and feeding of the calves. Her next job was cooking breakfast, whilst the older girls dressed the youngsters.

Breakfast usually consisted of *briwas* (a concoction of bread, a goodly lump of beef dripping and hot water – a very popular dish cooked in North Wales as late as 1960), or oatmeal as an alternative, tea, bread and butter, and bacon and egg for the men. The main meal of the day was at 12 noon, being mainly meat and two veg, plus a milky pudding.

All water was drawn from a well and carried. Clothes were hand washed or boiled in a cast-iron boiler, and irons were fire heated. Clothes were often handmade, and always by candlelight. Bread was baked in a Dutch oven. The interior of the oven was lined with bricks, dried gorse was packed inside and set alight and raked out when reduced to ashes, leaving the bricks red hot. The prepared loaves were quickly packed inside, the door closed and the cracks around the door sealed with spare dough so the heat could be maintained.

What bread! My mouth waters at the thought of it. Once the bread was removed, the rice pudding went in and cooked on the residual heat. The pudding emerged thick and creamy, better by half than modern puddings cooked in today's stoves, so my informant assured me. Again – yummy, yummy!

On top of all these chores, Anne Jane was expected to drop everything when Joseph required help sawing, for he allowed no one but his wife to man the pit end of the cross-cut saw. The two sawed in unison all the timber needed for wheels, shafts for carts, parts for furniture and planks for coffins. In an era when hard work was the order of the day, there is no doubt that these two were outstanding, for they reared ten children to well past adulthood at a time when diseases were rife and rampant, and hygiene practically nonexistent.

Of the two, Joseph was the more gifted. With little or no education he relied on rule of thumb to work out the adjustments needed for making wheels and building houses. He was also scrupulously honest, a sidesman at St Benedict's, Gyffin, on Sundays, and never bothered to hide his contempt when he heard of a shady or unfair deal. Two stories which highlight this have been handed down.

Like most men he enjoyed a pint, and one night in his local in Gyffin he met the owner of the the Oakwood Park Hotel, Mr James Stott, who often employed Joseph and his sons on a contract basis. On this particular night tempers on both sides were short and Joseph didn't have a shock of red hair for nothing, so bingo, fisticuffs resulted. After a good ding-dong they departed, one with a black eye and the other with a cut lip. No one present had an inkling about the motive for the fight, but Joseph was unrepentant. Next morning, farm chores proceeded as usual. About mid-morning a stocky figure was seen trudging up the drive. It was Mr Stott, to order some new wheels and shafts for a governess cart.

Another similar occasion arose some years later. This time the Hendre Bach farmer was contracted to the hotel to repaint a section of the home farm. Hard at work, Joseph was suddenly confronted by an irate James Stott who berated him soundly. Hey presto, and the paint pot landed square on the hotel owner's head. Again no one seemed to know the rights or wrongs of the argument, but next morning when Mr Stott appeared at the farm, not a word was uttered about the previous day's row. Instead he paid over some money and requested the men continue with the painting until it was finished. Was Joseph in the right on both counts? It certainly appears so.

The farmer had a soft side to his cantankerous nature. He was very fond of children and one of his delights on a cold dark night in winter was to make a cauldron of treacle toffee (*cyflath*) on the kitchen range, scrub scrupulously clean a floor slate and when fairly cold, he would roll the mixture into ropes and lay them to set on the clean slate. When it was ready each child was presented with a stick of toffee. One can picture the scene, a typical Victorian kitchen with the usual fire range and several small faces agog with pleasure and excitement anticipating the treat to come. Children at that time had so little, I doubt there was one toy in the whole house.

Joseph's penchant for honesty knew no bounds, for although extremely sympathetic where the local poor were concerned, they robbed his apple trees annually, and he more often than not waited months, if not years, for the payment of a coffin. However, if by chance he met a debtor in a public house, he would yell across the room, 'Hey you, what are you doing here? You owe me money.' Unfortunately, it is not known whether this blatant treatment produced results, but it was part of Joseph's philosophy.

Joseph died in 1922 aged 78 and Anne Jane died in 1928, also aged 78. Their sons continued to farm until the end of the war, when they decided to sell up. Their oldest child, a daughter named for her mother, married John Williams of Hendre Fawr, and they were my husband's grandparents. There are about 15 descendants living in Conwy and the valley but many more across the UK and worldwide.

Joseph and Anne Jane were typical Welsh farmers of the Victorian era who accepted life as it came, and became perfectionists because this gave them the satisfaction and spur to exist in a hard environment practically devoid of luxury and colour. They loved the simple things and were lucky enough to farm in a valley of immense beauty.

11

Sally Roberts

Our house at Groesffordd possessed only a stamp of a garden, and John, who was a very keen gardener, took to tending a large plot at Tyddyn Melus. As he was a very busy man, the weeding and hoeing became my responsibility.

So on most sunny days I would saunter down to my mother-in-law's, but I seldom got as far as the garden. A cup of tea and a tempting scone would be waiting, for my eager ear was needed to listen to the lonely old lady's tales of long ago. She was a wonderful storyteller, and I was enthralled and so very interested in the history of her early life, which had been arduous, deprived and extremely sad.

It was nearing Easter in the year 1890 and all the little girls in the village of Rhiwlas near Bangor were in a ferment of excitement, for this was the time for new clothes. All were expecting stunning new frocks, new dresses to adorn their pretty, petite figures when they attended chapel on Easter Sunday. The local dressmaker was busy and her hand sewing machine sang from morning till night, for not only did she have to please fussy, dictatorial mothers, but the coppers earned were the sole means of support for herself, her mother and small daughter Sally.

Sally went to chapel too, and she wanted a new frock. Bet, her mother, sat up late on Easter Saturday night, creating something special from pretty material left over from a larger garment, but sleep beckoned and the hem was only loosely tucked.

At chapel next day, after the service, the new frocks were duly admired. Sally, like all children, was hopping and skipping about and forgot the hem. Her foot caught in it, and down it came, hanging in tatters around her legs. Her slightly jealous companions laughed in glee, and poor Sally ran home in tears.

Sally Roberts, my mother-in-law, was born on 19th November 1885, the only child of Hugh and Elizabeth Roberts. Hugh was the local *crud* (shoemaker) and primarily made boots for the quarry miners. One day when Sally was three, Hugh delivered some boots to an outlying farm on the far side of Snowdon. It was late in the year, and the notorious mountain mist descended. Hugh, obeying local folklore, sat on a rock until the fog lifted. Drenched and frozen, he returned home to a sick bed and died from pneumonia a fortnight later.

After Hugh's death, Sally's mother Elizabeth continued her local dressmaking, carrying her faithful sewing machine from large house to mansion, carrying out any sewing job that needed doing. Meanwhile Sally was left with her *nain* (grandmother). Life in Rhiwlas was good, for it was a very happy village and the community spirit was strong. The chapel claimed every spare moment, singing was paramount, with choir practices, competitions and services almost every night.

Sally attended her local school, which was a national school, instead of the more usual church schools that were evident in most British communities at that time. When she related these events to me, she was in her late 70s and still had a vivid memory. I was interested to know if she had encountered the practice of the 'Welsh Not' during her schooldays, but she assured me she had not. It was the custom in most North Wales schools at that time to punish children who dared to lapse into their mother tongue instead of speaking English, the official language, by placing a board with the words 'Welsh Not' painted in vivid colours round their necks. The unfortunate victim was then encouraged to pass it on to the next culprit. At the end of the day the last hapless child was caned. Apparently Rhiwlas was one community where the Welsh language reigned supreme: everyone spoke Welsh freely, and the school taught no other language. Consequently Sally was never very happy speaking English, even though I and two of my children rarely spoke anything else.

Some of Sally's reminiscences were extremely colourful and of a time long gone; here is just one such anecdote. There were gypsy caravans in nearby woods and the children were Sally's playmates. They fascinated her, and she soulfully watched as the women carefully packed caked mud around the spines of a hedgehog and baked it on the edge of a fire. Then she quickly ran home in case she was asked to partake in the delicacy. This happy, carefree life continued until Sally was eleven, when tragedy struck again.

When she was eleven her mother died; overwork, everybody said. Her grandmother had passed away several years before, so the little girl was entirely on her own except for her mother's many brothers and sisters. One of them took charge of her and placed her in service to a bank manager. Just imagine, losing your adored mother, and then being sent to work as a skivvy at eleven years old. This was tragedy indeed, for she was a clever child and her mother dearly wanted her to become a pupil teacher, and then a teacher. But, alas, it wasn't to be.

Life at the bank manager's was dreary, and Sally often went hungry as food was doled out grudgingly. The work was hard, and when she complained to her uncle he found her a slightly more desirable situation in a large house near Llanrwst. This was as kitchen maid. The cook and housekeeper were very knowledgeable people and taught Sally well. She said she enjoyed working in that kitchen, and it was here that she decided she would be a cook. The household consisted of a retired Army officer, his family and grandchildren, whom Sally cooked for. She was responsible for all the nursery meals, which although basic, were embellished and decorated lavishly. For instance, one of the favourite recipes consisted of minced rabbit squeezed into small rabbit moulds, removed when firm, and set in aspic jelly. Rice puddings and other simple dishes were served in fancy dishes, and mashed potato was piped into small animal shapes.

The gentleman of the house was a martinet, a true British Army officer. All the servants stood to attention when speaking to him and were treated like second-class citizens. Everything had to shine, and everyone attended church on Sunday morning no matter what denomination they belonged to.

One summer the family went abroad and the servants let their hair down. All the best rooms were used, the Colonel's cigars were smoked, and the wine cellar was raided. Sally was fearful of the outcome, but after the servants had given the house a good thorough clean, and rearranged the stocks of food, everything appeared as normal when the family returned home. Sally stayed there for a year or two and then, deciding she wanted a change, took a post as chambermaid at a convalescent home for ladies in Llandudno Junction.

This home was run by an institution called the Birmingham Saturday Fund, funded by Midland firms for the use of their sick employees. Sally stayed for eight happy years until her marriage in 1915.

One unforgettable incident happened whilst she was a chambermaid, a situation that only lasted a short while, for when the cook left, Sally replaced her. Cleaning a bathroom one day, she suddenly looked down and saw that her skirt and knees were alive with lice. Panicking, she rang the alarm bell for help. Matron came running, took one look, and filled the bath with water and told Sally to get in. Meanwhile she gathered together the infected clothes and burnt them in the boiler. Clean and somewhat mollified, Sally returned to her duties. The Matron, a very kind-hearted woman, had a problem. Clearly one of the recuperating guests had a head full of lice, but she now had to detect the culprit and isolate her without divulging her identity. All these women were recovering from serious illnesses, and many came from slums where living conditions, by today's standards, were intolerable. The resident nurse very quietly inspected all the rooms and soon found the guilty party, who spent a day or two in the sick bay with none of her companions being any wiser.

The kitchens were typically Victorian and Sally soon mastered the art of cooking for large numbers. As was the habit of that time, a large stock pot boiled incessantly on the kitchen range and suet puddings were boiled in the copper boiler in the laundry.

About a mile away in Conwy, every Sunday evening in the summer, community hymn singing took place on an outcrop of rock attached to the eastern end of Telford's suspension bridge, known locally as Yr Ynys (the island). It was here one evening that Sally met her future husband Hugh John Williams, my father-in-law. His family kept a farm on the fringe of Conwy, and he and Sally married in 1915.

At first they lived in a rented cottage, but on the death of her husband's aunt, she and Hugh moved into the farmhouse at Hendre to keep house for the remaining family, Hugh's father and uncle. They lived here for 12 years, but during the slump in the 1920s, the uncle decided to retire, for he was in his late sixties (Hugh's father having died some time before), and move to a cottage they owned. They moved in 1927, my husband being five and a half years old and his sister, two and a half. This cottage is now my home, Tyddyn Melus, and although two new extensions have been added, it would be possible to remove the modern rooms and leave the cottage as it was at the time of George III.

Hugh died in 1963, and Sally soldiered on. When she was about 70 she became ill with Addison's disease, a rare cortisone deficiency, but once the right medication was prescribed she recovered quickly, and only one other hiccup occurred before she died.

One day about 1970, I had a frantic phone call; could I go to Tyddyn Melus as soon as possible? When I arrived, the old lady was in a terrible state with all the symptoms of food poisoning. Refusing to let me call the doctor, she deteriorated at an alarming rate. On the second day I ignored her pleas and medical help arrived. Immediately the hospital was mentioned, but this brought a downright refusal from the bed, with the added rider that there were plenty of people to look after her at home. Yes! One – yours truly.

As Sally was badly dehydrated, it was essential to set up a liquid drip to replace the fluid lost. A convenient nail on the wall was soon utilised, and a smart uniformed nurse was in attendance. However, the nurse had other calls, and after installing the apparatus she left, leaving me with her phone number and strict instructions to call if anything went wrong.

There was I, a complete greenhorn at nursing, faced with a complicated procedure ahead of me, but needs must when the devil drives, and my first consideration was my patient's flailing arms. The drip tube connection was reinforced by a piece of board strapped to the patient's wrist, and Sally in her comatose state was in danger of uncoupling the vital tube as her wrist moved violently over the bedclothes. There was only one solution: I must sit by the bed and hold the arm steady. The doctor had also mentioned that it was vital to ensure that the junction of tube and wrist was kept warm. This was essential for the smooth flow of the serum.

After about three hours, when my thirst and hunger became acute, Gwena, my daughter, a student, arrived at the same time as my husband with a large bag of fish and chips. I was still caressing the arm and unable to move, so Gwena fed me and I managed a drink with my left hand.

After a hiccup when the liquid refused to flow and the nurse was located at a Christmas party, the procedure was finally concluded at 2 a.m. next morning when the drip was removed by the doctor. We all drank a welcome cuppa and went to bed. Sally recovered and lived another ten years. She died when she was almost 90, after slipping on a loose mat.

Elizabeth Roberts's sewing machine, now almost 140 years old, is still working and occasionally used by her namesake and grand-daughter, my sister-in-law Elizabeth Davies, known to everyone as Betty. Whenever I see it I remember Sally's words, 'That sewing machine was a father to me.'

12

Cymro

From under a wriggling, whirling mass of moving fur, a small face appeared below two erect black ears. With some difficulty the face parted painfully from his brother and sisters, resisting all their joyful overtures for further play, and waddled his tiny body in my direction, pawing at my ankles for me to pick him up, which I did with alacrity. Once ensconced, he was mine and I was his, forever.

We called him Cymro, meaning 'Welshman', after a dog my husband had loved as a child. Cymro was a tiny Jack Russell; even fully grown he was a small dog for the breed. Somewhere, sometime, someone had told me that these small dogs were the clowns of the canine world, and our new dog was no exception. In fact, he was the King Clown. His antics were never planned, sometimes devastating, always hilarious. He enriched the lives of our family for eleven years.

He came to us in 1965, and at that time my husband John and I were living in a terraced house at Groesffordd, a hamlet near Conwy, with our children Gwena, 19, Hugh, 16, and Richard, 11. We moved to John's family smallholding, just a few hundred yards nearer Conwy, when his mother died in 1975. Cymro was ten and ailing, and he only lived at Tyddyn Melus for one year.

The house at Groesffordd had a magnificent view but was cold and always draughty. The garden was small, and the soil substandard, so little would grow. John, a keen gardener, gave up trying to cultivate it and grew oodles of vegetables in his mother's large garden. Our children roamed endlessly throughout the smallholding and neighbouring farms, enjoying an idyllic childhood in a neighbourhood that was traditionally theirs, for John's family had always lived in Hendre. I traced their roots in a direct line to 1400 and reckoned the line went back to the Domesday Book and farther, for the farming community moved little before cheap transport transformed the countryside. This glorious green sliver of Wales is loved by us all. John's sister Betty regularly brought her young family for weekends and holidays from their home in Chester, and Tyddyn Melus is still the centre of all our lives.

Cymro settled in very well, but like every animal, humans included, he was an individual and completely self-centred. As he was so small – the runt of the litter – his preferred mode of travel was to tuck himself into my coat with just his white face and two black ears protruding. 'Is that a Chihuahua?' I was frequently asked. But to be frank, I have never seen a Chihuahua so was unable to tell if Cymro resembled one or not.

At that time we just slept and ate at Groesffordd and tolerated the cold, characterless terrace house because of its proximity to John's mother, Nain to my children and Betty's, who at 80-plus, although fiercely independent, needed family attention.

The smallholding dwelling is situated at the side of the road, and was then and still is easily accessible to all and sundry. The family as a whole was reluctant to allow Nain to sleep there alone after the death of her husband, so Hugh and Richard took turns to stay with her overnight. One night when Richard was fast asleep in the tiny top bedroom, which was reached by a ladder, Cymro, who had accompanied him, started barking. Nain, looking through the window, saw a couple of strange men and promptly opened the door. Cymro tore out, barking vociferously, and took to the chase.

Richard, ignoring the ladder and jumping to the floor, joined the dog, but the men had disappeared. Nain, visibly shaken, but as resourceful as ever, quietly put on the kettle to make tea.

How many thousands of times has this act been performed in homes all over Britain, when accidents, frights and dark deeds have taken place? After the 'calming cup', the pair retired once again. Next morning, in John's 2-foot-high potato bed, a flat patch about 6-foot square was discovered, and it seemed likely that the would-be thieves had hidden there to escape detection.

Much discussion among the family revealed that an elderly woman living in a similar cottage a few miles away had been bodily injured whilst thieves carried away her valued grandfather clock before her eyes. Our Nain was the proud possessor of a very fine grandfather clock.

Cymro grew slowly from the Chihuahua stage but was never very big, and it soon became obvious that his main purpose in life was to become an exhibitionist. Always he played to the gallery, and his doggy soul basked in the resultant applause and attention. With his growth, his mode of travel changed; again it was sensational, for he never walked, but rode draped round my neck – a living fur collar.

Never once during the eleven years of his life was Cymro ever put on a lead; he either travelled in a car, standing upright on Richard's motorbike (these journeys were confined to the few hundred yards between Tyddyn Melus and Groesffordd, for we were not sure if there was a legal penalty for this display of ingenuity), or riding regally a-high on someone's shoulders. When travelling in a vehicle, he had to see the road in front; this necessitated his two front feet being placed on the dashboard, whilst his back legs danced a tango on the front passenger seat of the often fast-moving car. He liked it best when I travelled in the passenger seat, for, standing on my knees, the distance between seat and dashboard was considerably less and reduced the number of times he fell to the floor. However, I was a most unwilling participant, for his perpetual dancing movement on my often raked knees caused acute pain, a fact that my small dog was completely unaware of.

Always when travelling on the shoulders of a pedestrian, he managed to convey to other dogs his utter contempt for their often contented but always docile obedience to the lead. They were considered of the lowest caste and generally treated with a disdainful glance and a short, snappy bark saying, 'You poor mutt; where's your brains?'

Unfortunately, Cymro had two besetting sins. He was fussy beyond belief about his food, and he left a watery trademark on a few of his favourite objects: a typewriter, one particular table leg, the corner of the kitchen stove and, favourite of all, a portable wireless, which he eventually put out of commission. This habit arose because he had a kidney problem and was unable to regulate himself. The Dettol bottle and pepper pot were in constant use.

Most dogs live for their food and have voracious appetites. Cymro never once ate with relish but treated all food with disdain. Tinned food of any kind was his pet abomination; one sniff, a flick of the tail and he was off, to eat no more that day. Fresh meat and chicken liver were tolerated but not enjoyed. The exception to this self-imposed fast was an occasional pear, when pips, flesh and core all vanished in a blink of an eye. Food was just not important, but excitement was, and if the family couldn't provide him with this very necessary active emotion, he'd be off down rabbit holes, nosing along the river bank, or ratting in one of the open sheds. His happiest times were spent at Tyddyn Melus, playing with the boys, swinging from a bicycle inner tube suspended high in a large apple tree. To get full enjoyment from this exercise, a full-blown charge was needed; he would start halfway down the garden and run towards his goal at full speed, finally jumping many times his own height to embed his teeth in the tube. Suspended thus, he would swing happily for a few minutes, and then the whole procedure would be repeated time and time again.

The *pièce de résistance* of his repertoire was undoubtedly the sledge-hammer tableau. Hugh, Richard and their friends gathered regularly every Sunday morning at the smallholding to chat and mend their old cars. Cymro was, of course, a prime attraction and the boys' happy merriment at his quaint antics could be heard a mile away. In the beginning the lads threw sticks for Cymro to retrieve but this was too ordinary for our laddo, and one day, spotting a large sledgehammer that had been left carelessly on the ground, he carried the heavy object and placed it carefully at Hugh's feet. Laughing heartily, Hugh threw it as far as he could, never thinking the little dog could carry the heavy object all that distance. But our hero dutifully fetched the sledgehammer and once again proudly presented it to one of the boys.

What was really amazing was the tiny dog's obvious enjoyment from the whole procedure. He would sit listening to the mirth all around him, then paw at the trousers of the nearest boy, eager for another go.

When the sledgehammer was banished by grown-ups fearful for the health of their ingenious pet, sticks being considered beneath his contempt, large logs and branches were brought from all quarters of the small farm – and presented with little finesse to whoever he considered most likely to oblige him by tossing the object as far away as possible. There was obviously no fun to be had if the task was easy. Large stones, too, were grist to the mill, and after we moved and were building an extension, John and the boys would put stones in the cement mixer after use with water to clean it. Cymro, deprived of what he considered his property, would slink into the whirling mixer, to be rescued, dripping wet and filthy, by a laughing boy.

There was no end to his tricks when the boys were mending cars and motorbikes; bushes, nuts, washers, bolts, spanners and screwdrivers would vanish. A cry would be heard, 'Have you seen a half-inch spanner?' and our chap would be seen on the horizon, burying the trophy.

For Christmas one year Richard bought him a dog's rubber newspaper with a built-in squeak. It was very well made, and dog and newspaper developed a love–hate relationship. Not really knowing what the object was – maybe a mouse, it sounded like a mouse, but a mouse didn't have a plastic-ky feel, it had fur – Cymro subjected it to some very devastating attacks. He tried shaking it violently, and it still roared disturbingly; he bit it endlessly and the noise endured; he threw it in the air time over time, and the loud 'peep-peep' was still audible. He then stopped and took stock, finally resorting to a medley of all three mediums, and eventually the poor tortured object flew into bits. Cymro, having successfully 'killed it', resumed his usual recumbent position in front of the fire.

When he was eight or nine years old he developed a penchant for rubber; it was his delicacy. Not for him a juicy bone or flavoursome dinner, he chewed delightedly on a rubber washer or a piece of eraser. All this became a terrible nightmare, for he swallowed the rubber often in large chunks, and it didn't take much imagination to know that this didn't do very much for his digestive system. It culminated in a terrible accident.

It happened one summer Sunday when John was busy with an electric drill in his workshop at Tyddyn Melus. At that time the only access to the mains supply was in the house, so a long cable was necessary. Services, e.g. water, sewage and electricity (gas being out of the question), were at a premium as John's mother, who was well into her eighties, refused all her children's overtures to modernise the cottage. John, engrossed and busy with the implement he was mending, failed to see mi-laddo gnawing away at the rubber cable.

All of a sudden there was an earth-rending flash, and a little black and white bundle rolled over and over, through the door and halfway down the garden, coming to rest, completely out, in a bed of nettles.

A startled son and dazed husband picked up the rigid figure who, although deeply concussed, was breathing shallowly. They massaged his chest vigorously, watched over by an anxious crowd of youngsters. Suddenly one black eye opened and with one jerk, he was up and away, biting furiously at the wire, anxious to kill the demon that had attacked him. Needless to say, eager hands pulled him to safety. Foiled from his desperate task, spitting and growling, he finally succumbed to the petting and, as always, played to the gallery – for wasn't he Cymro, the star performer?

On at least two other occasions, he was determined to annihilate the bogeyman inhabiting the cable and made straight for the wire on entering the workshop. Luckily, on both occasions, a large hand was available to stop his shenanigans.

Is there any other animal alive with eyes so expressive as a dog? They are usually large and very velvety; Cymro's were small and bead-like. But all have that desperate, haunting, pleading look, expressing unique emotions. He never used his eyes for purely selfish motives, unlike our more recent dogs, for he never needed favours of any kind. All he required from humans was adulation and laughter. He was in seventh heaven when an audience applauded his desperate exploits. Also unlike most of his kind, he had little capacity for either loyalty or love. He liked me, but my affection for him was never fully reciprocated, and the rest of the family were taken for granted.

His attitude to other dogs was also rather odd, neither liking nor disliking them. They would approach him with either hectic tail-wagging or a snide snarl, and all he showed was static indifference, standing statue-like while they sniffed his face and nether parts, and disdainfully walking away when they had finished, with unfeigned boredom. Only once did he ever fight, preferring caution, which usually meant running away as fast as his legs would carry him. This in itself was unusual behaviour for a Jack Russell, for most of them enjoy a good, violent scrap.

Two or three doors away from us, there lived a very large Red Setter, a fairly peaceful dog, whose sole excitement at 8.30 every morning was to chase Cymro along our cul-de-sac and into our house. The little dog treated this disturbance with his usual indifference, settling down in front of the fire on his return. One morning, however, Red must have been feeling either vindictive or out of sorts, for after the usual chase he sank his fangs into the Jack Russell's heels.

Bang! Crash! Wallop! The terrier turned, all indifference gone; with every hair upright, he became Attila the Hun in the twinkling of an eye. With Red to the right, and Red to the left of him, he fought savagely and did the terrier population proud. Red hair flew everywhere, and whimpers hit the air. Diving for the legs and biting brutally, he was a round ball of vicious intent, snarling, barking, darting and gnawing dangerously on all four of the large, gangling, spindly legs. Red tried to retaliate but his opponent was quicksilver, a shifting, elusive target, and all because the large dog had made the terrible mistake of thinking the small dog was all coward. The noise was deafening and brought noses to windows. After a lifetime of just two minutes, Red limped away, frightened, cowed and thoroughly whipped. Cymro, unhurt, swaggered his tiny, taut body, alive with throbbing, exultant success. After wagging his stub of a tail at me, he retired to the fireside, 'King of the Jungle'.

All his lifting of heavy weights and continual punishing exercise took its toll. He became listless, and when he tried to take part in his old activities his legs wouldn't carry him. Over the years he had made many visits to the vet, who always tied up Cymro's nose before investigating, saying in an ominous voice, 'I have met your type before.' On the last occasion, the poor lad, too ill to remonstrate in the usual canine manner, pleaded with his two expressive eyes, 'I'll be good, Mister, I'll be good', but this was the end, the time had come to say goodbye. The ingested rubber and the carrying of objects twice his weight had taxed his tiny heart, and I knew I had to say the word, to put him to rest and end his torment.

I carried him home and buried him in the garden, a never, ever to be forgotten, mad, courageous, tenacious little dog.

13

One Thoughtless Moment

January is always a dreary month, and the year 1969 was no exception. But on the morning of the 14th I awoke excited, for John had three days' holiday from his job as a sales and service manager in an agricultural engineering firm situated 20 miles away in St Asaph. We planned to go out and about and take my mother-in-law with us; she was 84 years old and lived alone in the traditional family home where my family now live, a quarter of a mile down the lane from where I lived with John and my two teenaged sons, Hugh and Richard. My daughter Gwena was in college at that time.

The morning was dull and overcast, but dry, so we decided to go ahead with our plans. John would spend the morning completing work on a new drive at his mother's house, and I would make dinner and finish the daily household chores, leaving the afternoon free for our trip out.

Halfway through the morning, the phone rang, and it was one of John's salesmen, wanting some urgent information. Rather than phoning his elderly mother, who had a very slippy muddy walk to reach John, I turned off the washing machine, checked the meat in the oven, and started off down the lane. I heard a car coming but as I was well tucked into the hedge, I didn't worry. The next thing I knew through a pain-filled fog was John and some locals standing over me with worried faces and a reassurance that the ambulance was coming.

John, working just below his mother's house, heard a horrific loud bang, and fearing a car had crashed into his parked vehicle, ran up the lane to behold a bundle of rags in the ditch, and a car leaving the scene. He immediately ran up to the driver and demanded where he was going.

'To get the police,' the man replied.

'Well! Don't you think we'd better find out who it is?' John said, never dreaming I was the victim. He had the shock of his life when my face stared blankly up at him.

The ambulance didn't arrive for nearly an hour, and it began to drizzle. The pain was so bad that I drifted in and out of consciousness. When we finally got to the hospital the emergency staff were so kind and efficient, and in no time I was warm and dry, my broken leg reasonably comfortable in a splint. My face had suffered badly, for apparently I had been dragged along before the car halted. There was a jagged triangular tear over my left eye and numerous dotted cuts and bruises, and my whole countenance resembled a mummified pig's.

Everything healed splendidly except the broken leg; nearly ten months after the event it was still encased in plaster. John came home one evening to find me newly returned from a hospital visit with yet another, larger cast. He blew. 'I want another opinion!' he yelled. Up to that time I had been under the care of a general surgeon at nearby Llandudno Hospital, as my injury was not considered serious enough for reference to an orthopaedic specialist, even though it had been deemed necessary to insert a plate in my ankle.

After much persuasion, for the surgeon insisted that only time would repair my leg, we secured an appointment with Mr Robert Owen – now Sir Robert Owen – at that time an up-and-coming orthopaedic surgeon. After tests he assured me that time was not a factor, for if it had been, my leg would have healed. He operated, and gave me 30 years' more walking time until the dreaded arthritis descended on my badly impaired leg. I am now very disabled and walk with crutches, but after two major accidents I count myself very lucky.

I will never forget my first visit to that clinic. There was no one-to-one consultation: I entered a roomful of small children, all with metal squares strapped to their feet. I was told later that none of these youngsters could walk properly and the contraptions they were wearing had been devised by the consultant and his workforce.

I admired the man from that moment on, and even more next day when I was awaiting the result of my X-ray. I could hear the surgeon on the phone in the next room, speaking urgently to someone, asking them to check on an old pensioner neighbour, for when he had passed her house that morning the curtains had not been drawn, and there was no one about. This was a very busy man, and he still was human enough to have concern for a very elderly lady.

On the morning of my operation, which was due at 1 p.m., news percolated into the ward that the boss was in a foul mood, and that he had sacked all the porters for minor errors, for he was a perfectionist and expected the same high standards he set himself from his staff. Late that evening, after operating for a full 12 hours, this most human man came to my bedside and told me he had found my leg in a terrible condition and that he had inserted a bone graft, and now we would have to let time do all the work. As I have mentioned previously, my leg did heal and I never saw the inside of a hospital again for 20 years.

A man as successful as Mr Owen was never going to remain for long in North Wales, and soon after my operation he moved to a Liverpool hospital and opened a private clinic in Rodney Street.

When in 1991 my arthritis was badly affecting both knees, I again consulted Mr Owen, hoping he would consent to operating on me once more for knee replacements. However, this was not to be as he was bordering on retirement and had given up all NHS work. He recommended a good North Wales consultant who operated on both knees, giving me a painless future, if a rather stiff one.

Incidentally, Mr Owen never sent me a bill for that consultation, adding to my sheer admiration of the man. How many thousands of victims have privately worshipped their medical benefactors from afar, wishing there was some practical means other than a donation, which often is not possible, to show how grateful they are for the gift of extended life.

In my case it was 30 more years of walking freely, and it's only now at 85 when I am finally crippled that I realise how depressing those years would have been if John and I had listened to the Llandudno consultant. So Sir Robert, as he now is known, is revered by me along with my other hero, Winston Churchill.

I have just one other remembrance of this remarkable individual. Turning on the telly a year or two back, I saw a little Asian boy being operated on by my old doctor, now well into retirement. Listening to the programme, I found out that he at that time was spending part of every year in the Third World saving crippled children.

Before I leave this chapter, I will return to the man who ran me down all those years ago. Did he have any remorse for a moment's thoughtlessness; did he care that he literally changed my life?

14

Tyddyn Melus

When John, my husband, inherited our seventeenth-century Welsh cottage from his parents, it looked as idyllic and was as insanitary as when I first saw it 65 years ago during the war. The rough stone walls of the dwelling were brilliant white from countless coats of limewash. The windows were small and had an iron bar across each of the panes. In summer red and pink roses climbed in a traditional way round a squat green front door that opened onto a garden full of apple trees. Beyond the apple trees, a trout stream gurgled its way down from Tal-y-Fan mountain to the sea.

Through the open door, in the living-room a Welsh dresser resplendent with blue willow-ware china was to be seen, together with copper kettles, a corner cupboard and a grandfather clock as old as the house itself. But down a leafy path, tucked away in a matching white stone shed, was the chemical toilet; and in splendid isolation the solitary cold tap held court in an adjoining shed. John's mother lived to be 90 and felt she could not cope with the mess made by alterations, being quite content with conditions as they were.

Surrounding the house were approximately 4 acres of land, much of which was a peat bog, that were let to a cousin for sheep grazing. The whole property had been bought originally by John's great-great-grandfather, one William Williams, farmer, back in 1869 to retire to in his old age. Unfortunately, this never came about as the poor man suddenly died. Instead, the cottage (*tyddyn* in Welsh) provided a home for countless descendants who did little in the way of maintenance, for the attractive exterior hid a multitude of sins. And if, as we intended, our family of four were to live in it, much would have to be done to bring it up to standard.

Now the really sensible thing to do would have been to pull down the ruins and start from scratch, but this cottage was beloved by us all – by John who had been brought up here, by Hugh and Richard, our grown-up sons who had played here, and by myself because I love old things. So we decided to install all the essentials of modern living, whilst retaining as many of the old features as possible. The original building, which consisted of one fairly large single-storey living-room-cum-kitchen, a lower bedroom (*siamber*) and a small upper room (*lloft*), was to be rendered sound but left almost intact with only minor alterations, such as larger windows, plastered walls, damp courses, etcetera. The new extension would be simple so as to blend unobtrusively with the ancient cottage.

Another poser was the building grant. Government-aided local authority grants 33 years ago when we started the ball rolling were for 50 per cent of the cost or a maximum of £1600, and only paid when the work was finished and the building inspector satisfied that the property met modern-day requirements. A further condition specified that the whole undertaking must be carried out by a qualified builder. Sensibly, we took the problem to a local architect, who after inspecting the cottage assured us that the cost of work if carried out by a contractor would be in the region of £7000 or £8000. Phew! At the very least, we would have to find £6000. To take the grant or not to take the grant, was our sole topic of conversation for weeks. Reluctantly we finally decided against the handout, for in those days inflation was rife and labour was the expensive item and key factor. And we had a ready-made labour force of our own: John and the boys, being big, brawny and able, were willing to undertake all the unskilled and as much of the skilled work as they were capable of. Needless to say we were not entirely satisfied that our decision was the right one, until some of the work programme was completed and we realised just how much the building material cost without the added labour bill.

The next step was also a teaser: should we continue to rent our comfortable adjacent modern home until work at the cottage was completed, or should we burn our boats and move hook, line and sinker into the cottage for the sake of saving a few pounds a week? I was given the final word, and rightly or wrongly, I plunged for living on the job. So one hot June Sunday the boys hitched a trailer to the car and the Williams family were on the move. And I found myself in the same position as the 'old lady who lived in a shoe', only my trouble was too much furniture instead of too many children. As the outside buildings were even more rickety than the house itself, one of our first tasks was to erect a large shed to house our many possessions. Unfortunately, after a month or two the mice who had been living right royally in the rubble between the double stone walls of the house became homeless and invaded our new three-piece suite. Luckily the damage was spotted almost immediately, but some much begrudged capital was expended to wrap each individual item of furniture in a thick coating of plastic. This, plus regular inspections, kept the little rascals at bay. A corner of this shed also did duty as a workshop and houses our freezer which is filled during the summer months from our large vegetable plot.

It was finally decided to undertake the work in three stages. Priority was a septic tank (for we are far from a main drainage system), lavatory and bathroom. As the cottage was so small we were allowed to erect a small extension – provided it did not exceed a certain size – for these commodities without first obtaining planning permission. All that was needed was the architect's plan and the go-ahead from the local authority's housing department. The next step was the renovation of the original house, and the third operation would be a further extension of two bedrooms with the lower existing bedroom becoming a kitchen.

In the past, *tyddyns* such as ours peppered the uplands of Snowdonia. They were known as 'crog loft cottages' because the upper bedroom was reached by means of a movable ladder. When I married my husband in 1945, the family still used this ladder, but an unlucky tumble by my mother-in-law saw the advent of a cumbersome staircase that protruded into the living room and completely spoilt it. At that time the house was lit by paraffin lamps and water was carried from a pump on a nearby hill. Since then, water and electricity have been connected.

Settling in was a problem for a family of young moderns used to basking daily in a hot bath. My heart bled for my two water-loving sons who, when sticky, sweaty and dog-tired from digging and labouring, were forced to wash up as far as possible, and down as far as possible, with tepid water from a plastic bowl.

The weather that summer (1975) was glorious and the work went with a will: ditches were dug and the drains laid in no time, brick-layers were employed and the septic tank, bathroom and toilet became realities. By the end of September we were enjoying hot baths again, but in a building devoid of all decoration including the floor tiles. Oh! The sheer luxury of gallons of hot water and a clean body, even if pieces of plastic flapped eerily in the windows, and the dust from the concrete smothered one's clean feet.

By October the new building was nearing completion with just the twiddly bits left, and when the rains came it soon became evident that the *siamber* (downstairs bedroom) was more than a little damp. Now in my mother-in-law's day, an enclosed fire burned daily in this room, but it had been one of our first casualties as it took up too much space. So it became imperative that we proceeded immediately with the second stage of our programme – the complete renovation of the old house – instead of waiting for the better weather in the spring.

This meant that my already weary menfolk would not have a much-earned rest. With the rains came a bank statement and the realisation of the full cost of the project. From then on we were on our own; no longer could we afford the luxury of paid labour. Fortunately by this time all three were fairly competent. Richard, who worked in the building trade, was the bricklayer and drain expert. Hugh found the roof more to his liking and laid slates like an old hand, whilst John at 50 tackled the stone masonry of the old walls with an expertise reminiscent of an old-time stone mason. Also, it is only fair to say that without our many friends the whole operation would never have got off the ground. We were very lucky that the boys' pals included a plasterer and plumber, and John numbered among his friends a master builder who was ever ready with advice and material, his cousin Dick who had first-hand knowledge and, last but not least, Jim, who rewired the whole place and never charged us a bean.

So in the autumn the bare backs of summer were replaced with oilskins and wellingtons. The *siamber* was stripped. The floorboards put down by my father-in-law 40 years earlier were full of dry rot and on removal exposed a steady stream of water running right across the room. The work intensified, the floors and walls were drained, damp-proofed and concreted, the existing window was enlarged and another window was made in the 3-foot-thick walls to meet the light requirement. The old beams were scraped clean, treated with anti-woodworm serum and replaced, the walls were plastered and colour-washed. The upstairs room received similar treatment. This work took until January. During the early stages the rain was continual; the men dripped and stripped continually, but carried doggedly on.

The new extension was so packed up with heavy furniture that it was an adventure just to wash and bathe. As before, dust and plaster seeped everywhere. It was impossible to find anything and cries of, 'Mum, where's my socks?', 'Have you seen the large yellow screwdriver?' and 'Watch out! That's not safe!' were everyday occurrences.

Sleeping arrangements were sketchy, with sons dossing down on living-room floor and parents travelling 4 miles over a mountain to pregnant daughter's house to sleep, and all because the hi-fi equipment had pride of place in the caravan. Mud and dust coated everything, and it was at Christmas time that morale was at its lowest ebb, tempers being very frayed. So wisely we called a halt and spent the holiday with Gwena, our daughter, who lived at that time across the mountain, high up in Snowdonia. But things weren't too serene there, for Gwena gave birth to a great big beautiful boy on 29th December.

After the break it was back to the grindstone. Although I took little or no part in the building activities, my lot was far from easy, for hard-working men are hungry men and I was taxed to the hilt trying to provide mammoth meals in primitive surroundings. My washing-up bowl constantly disappeared, my buckets vanished during the first onslaught, and I caught glimpses of them occasionally, coated with cement or some similar slime. The washing-up liquid also took a walk from time to time, for apparently this substance ensures the pliability of a certain type of mortar. The climax came when preparing to attend an important function with my husband. I picked three pieces of plaster off my evening cape. When the bedrooms were finished, we unanimously voted against proceeding with the rest of the second stage. So we refurnished the bedrooms, removed the hi-fi equipment from its comfortable lodgings, washed and polished everything and everywhere, and enjoyed a much-earned rest. But not for long. Spring came and the garden beckoned.

For years now, whilst his mother was alive, John had cultivated a good piece of the bottom field as a garden and drained most of the peat bog. But this year, helped by the knowledge that potatoes in North Wales had hit the record price of 22p a pound, we decided to enlarge this plot. At Whitsun when everything was planted, one friend gave us part of an old glass house and another friend stumped up with a frame. In two days whilst on holiday John and Richard erected a very professional-looking greenhouse out of these two cast-outs, and although it was a bit late, we stocked it with tomato plants.

With 1976 following the pattern of the previous summer and becoming even hotter, we were loath to disturb the quiet evenness of our lives by restarting the second stage. June gave way to July and still we tarried, happily tending the garden and putting the early fruits and vegetables in the freezer. Then Hugh announced that he was beginning his fortnight's holiday on 24th July and was prepared to spend the first week getting started on the living room, the only room in the house as yet untouched. So three or four days beforehand I put away all my old Welsh china and brass and copper ornaments and other treasures.

This time we were determined to keep our living quarters completely separate from the alterations, and this with careful planning we managed to do. We ate in the caravan and washed and slept in the renovated part of the house, for everyone realised just how important it was to keep morale high. Nothing is more demoralising than living for months on end in confusion with nowhere to relax.

By the Tuesday of Hugh's holiday, the window was out, the door was out, the walls were stripped bare, and the Triplex stove lay sootily on its side beneath an apple tree. The stairs too had had their marching orders, for they spoilt the living room, and the boys were quite content to use a movable ladder as their ancestors did until we managed to build the new bedrooms.

Once the dross had been cleared the original hearth, simple and wide as always in houses of that era, displayed its hidden secrets, covered so long by many generations of fashion-conscious people always anxious to 'Keep up with the Joneses' of their time, forever despising the genuine original for gaudy, often gimmicky, modern installations. On the left-hand flank of the fireplace was an exquisitely round-domed bread oven complete with cracked old bricks, similar to the oven at Hendre Bach. These ovens were gorse fired and are to be found in all local houses built before the advent of the black lead stove. Sometimes in larger farms they were hidden away in an outhouse. When John was young his great-grandmother who lived on the next farm had an outdoor oven of this kind and used it regularly.

A second uncovered treasure was a cupboard, just left of the bread oven but higher and still near the fire. The interior is quite large and carefully lined with small stones untouched by lime mortar of any kind. At first we were at a loss to know the purpose of this cupboard, for similar cottages (mostly old ruins now) only possess the gorse oven. Then John and his cousin Bob (Dick's brother) found by looking at the outside wall that at one time there had been a corresponding aperture on the outside and it became clear that some commodity or other had been fed into the house from without. Bob, who was well into his seventies, suddenly remembered a cottage high up in the mountains near a peat bog, which had an identical cupboard. And we had a peat bog – or did once, for it was fast becoming reclaimed land. So we all agreed that peat was dried in this hole high up in the chimney wall; but just to make sure I showed a local historian who was also uncertain but agreed that our theory was probably the right one. Both these old features remain exposed in all their ancient glory, with just touches of modern restoration to preserve them for always.

Looking back, there were many anxious moments over those months, such as the time John tripped over a plank and strained his shoulder pretty badly. He seethed whilst he watched Hugh, who had taken his holiday at the same time as his father, tackle the roof on his own. And then there was the anthrax scare.

The old method of binding plaster for use between the roof beams just below the slates was to mix animal hair with lime mortar, and when our roof was being reslated, large quantities of this stuff fell about everywhere. One night while this was happening we were visited by our master builder friend, who was horrified.

'You'll get anthrax from that!' he said. 'Watch none of you cut yourselves.' He backed up his remark by saying that hair from infected animals was used indiscriminately in olden times, as nobody realised the danger. I was terrified and went round everywhere gingerly with a dustpan and brush, until my down-to-earth husband realised that the hot lime in the mortar would kill any germ. At least that was his theory, and I agreed with him and put my mind at rest. No one was any the worse, thank goodness, and a goodly amount of that old lime mortar was used to condition the soil round the winter's Savoy cabbages.

There were many funny moments, too. At the height of all the activity my old trusty washing machine packed up, and no one had time to look at it. I was faced with two alternatives: I could wash everything by hand or go to the launderette in Conwy and take my turn with the dozens of holidaymakers. I plumped for washing the articles myself, and hit on a bright idea. I sorted the clothes, put them in the bath, and paddled on them in the manner of the natives. They came surprisingly clean – clean enough anyway to be dirtied again by plaster or car oil, for my lads are car mad as well as hi-fi enthusiasts. Whilst tackling this task I was so absorbed that I failed to hear the arrival of two post office engineers who had come to repair the telephone. They called out, and not receiving any reply they walked through the open door into the hall and peeped into the nearest room. Imagine their surprise when they beheld a middle-aged woman with greying hair stomping up and down in the bath, fully clothed but with bare feet. Being very nice young men they turned away, but one could not control himself and started to laugh. Then I laughed and explained the situation. They mended the phone and left, but I am quite sure they thought I was a little mad to behave in such a way in this day and age.

Another funny episode occurred when the living room was open to the sky and the boys were so busy that they were unable to indulge in their usual Sunday morning drink with their friends. Whilst they were working, one waggish friend hung a topical plaque on a ladder that read, 'Work is the curse of the drinking classes'. That plaque will remain in that room forever, even if it clashes most horribly with my old furniture.

During the hot summer our vegetables, unlike our neighbours', flourished. John, foreseeing another summer like 1975, had well mulched all our crops with manure, which acted as a sponge as well as being a fertilizer, and retained the moisture. After filling the freezer I was left with a surplus of both vegetables and fruit, so I erected a sign and sold the remainder. Holidaymakers from nearby caravan sites and locals behaved like true Britons and wended their way through piles of rubble stones and broken slates to buy a fresh lettuce or a pound of beans. However, the vegetables must have tasted good for they returned time and time again, and I was kept busy picking the produce whilst the men slogged away on the roof.

With the roof and outside door off, I had another worry. The boys' bedroom – the old crog loft – was exposed, and my old friend, the cosseted hi-fi equipment, was open to view and at the mercy of any small-time crook. Every time I left the house, which was as little as possible during that period, I carefully climbed the ladder and covered the precious objects with a blanket, putting planks against the open doorway plus a wheelbarrow full of bricks. All to save articles that were at times the bane of my existence as the boys, like most youngsters, possessed rubber ears and were unable to enjoy any music unless it was played deafeningly loud.

As I have already made clear, all this happened in the 1970s when I was but 50 and my now 50-plus sons were in their twenties. But I dreamily remember one Sunday when the roof was being renovated, and the bath water had started running and would not stop until four filthy workers were clean once more. It was getting dusk outside and through the *siamber* window I could dimly see the piles of slates, ready for finishing the roof on the morrow.

Thirty years on, and the cottage and garden are still beloved by our whole family. All that hard graft has stood the test of time, and the old walls never let in a drop of water or even a hint of dampness. A further extension was added about ten years ago, and we now have two new bedrooms. The living room is bereft of its cooking section, the *siamber* has become an up-to-date kitchen, and overall we are more comfortable. Unfortunately, only my youngest son and I live here now as Hugh married Theodora in 1985 and John, my husband, died in 2004. But Hugh and Richard are partners in an engineering concern situated on our property, and both still eat me out of house and home. (Bless them!)

15

Dilys, Houdini and the Swimming Sheep

On a stormy night 30-odd years ago triplet lambs were born to a middle-aged Welsh mountain ewe. Two of the lambs died soon after birth, but the third, a poor misshapen scrap of animal life, survived and we christened her Dilys. From an early age it became clear that Dilys would be unable to live the normal life of a mountain sheep, for not only was she pot-bellied and very small, but her knees were swollen and she walked with a strange jerking gait.

Dilys was a member of a very compact flock of mountain sheep, about a hundred in number (without the yearly lambs), owned by two Welsh brothers known locally as Dick and Bob Farm, who were my husband's cousins. For months at a time the flock lived and roamed the mountainside, existing on the short sweet grass and practising the expertise bred into the flock by their forebears. The peaks of Snowdonia are notoriously dangerous and, although many a Welsh ewe has been killed by speeding motorists on the bordering main roads, very few fall into the hundreds of pitfalls and crevasses. Narrow paths made by sheep can be seen on the rockiest surface and visitors to the area are often alarmed when they see one of these hardy animals, probably with a lamb or two, poised on a rocky promontory with a steep drop on one side.

The sheep were only brought to the farm fields for lambing, shearing, dipping, etcetera. The brothers used the two meadows adjacent to my home for this purpose, and it was in our upper field that Dilys was born. Although Bob and Dick were aware from the start of Dilys's infirmity, neither had the heart to ask the vet to terminate her life. So she grazed contentedly in our fields, totally free from the attentions of the rams of the flock. She was not expected to live through her first winter but she soldiered on, probably because the weather was so mild. Like an only child she soon became spoilt, and even the two dogs treated her as a special case. When the other sheep were in the field, Dilys was never rounded up and counted with the rest but left in peace in the ruins of an old shed which she had adopted as a hiding place and shelter. If for some reason her presence was required, half-blind, half-deaf Robin, who suffered from a congenital disease handed down to him from a one-time Scottish champion sheepdog, eased her gently from her hidey-hole as if he was fully aware of her infirmity. Dilys, of course, made capital of this situation and swaggered more pointedly than usual as she delicately picked her way in front of the dog.

Now it is a recognised thing that sheep are stupid. But like many humans, as any farmer will tell you, sheep like their own way, and it takes a determined man and dog to make sure they do not get it. Most sheep have largish faces with vacant eyes, but the Welsh mountain breed have pretty pointed faces with most intelligent eyes, and Dilys was no exception.

All of us – that is, Bob and Dick, my husband and myself – agreed that Dilys really had a beautiful, mobile face, and like all handsome females, she made full use of it; she gazed at you with wistful eyes until, full of compassion, you'd pick an apple or pluck a tasty green morsel from the garden and hold it out for her to peck daintily at. If in haste you tossed the apple to her, Dilys would place her two sore front knees on the grass before grudgingly eating the apple, as a protest, instead of bending normally as if she was grazing. This kneeling habit was a favourite trick and was done to elucidate her sorry plight. The annoying thing was that we were all perfectly aware that we were being conned, but were so full of admiration for her guile that she was rewarded. A real con-sheep if ever there was one.

During one sweltering summer, the spring in the top field, like so many more during that unusually hot period, completely dried up and water had to be carried from our house across the road. While the other sheep waited patiently for the containers to be filled, Madame Dilys demanded instant attention and insisted upon drinking straight from the bucket. She soon learned when to expect one of us with the buckets and was always waiting at the gate.

This chore, however, did not go on for long because the field which is on an incline soon became tasteless tinder under the daily relentless sun, and Dilys, with her friends, was moved to our bottom field which, under normal conditions, is part peat bog. This pasture is bounded by a small river and is barely an acre in size, but it was greener than any other field in the locality even though 42 sheep grazed it for six or seven weeks. Amongst the 42 were lambs fattening for the September sales, and whilst other farmers were carrying food and water to their sheep, ours thrived and were very little the worse for the hot weather.

Amongst these sheep was a full-grown ewe known as Split Ear, so-called because Robin tore her ear when she was a lamb. She was as wily as Dilys but without her charm. Woe betide any one of us who accidentally left open the gate leading from the garden to this pasture, for Split Ear was soon through and munching at my prize caulis. We took a fairly lenient view of this because of the small amount of nutrition in the grass; in fact, we regularly took large quantities of unwanted green stuff into the field. Not all the sheep were keen on these handouts, but those that were came running the moment anyone appeared with an armful of greenery. The others ate the grass between the reeds in the peat bog which never quite dried up all summer. Broad bean leaves were the favourite with the weed fat hen a close second. Split Ear herself was very partial to lettuce that had run to seed, while Dilys stuck doggedly to apples.

We had another joker among the sheep whose name speaks torrents: Houdini, and no fence or hedge could hold her. One day she escaped during lambing time, and that worried the brothers because the sheep are always kept close at hand when the lambs are due. She was eventually found during the summer with a very large, very healthy lamb, not on the mountain as everyone expected, but on a hill farm 3 miles distant.

Brought home in disgrace, she soon had the hedges in our top field in shreds, and I was kept busy rescuing her and her lamb. In desperation we placed her in the lower pasture in the hope that the still moist grass would satisfy her and stem her wanderlust. But no, in no time at all she was fording the tiny trickle of water that struggled to flow between the dry caked mud of the river bed, taking with her eight or nine other sheep. It then became a daily routine to send the dogs across the stream to a neighbouring farmer's property to round up the culprits. Sometimes they were fields away and Dick had to fetch them back by road. On one occasion the neighbour, a friend of ours, brought the wanderers back himself. I was most apologetic for grass was scarce everywhere, but he told me not to worry, for all the sheep and cattle in the district were roaming, trying to search out eatable fodder.

A couple of months later the rains got under way in earnest. Now it was the policy of the brothers and most other farmers of the area to sell the four-year-old ewes to lowland farmers, as by that age the teeth have started to rot and the animals are unable to chew the short mountain grass, but will live for some time in places where there is longer, more fertile grass.

On the second Monday in September the old ewes were sent to market and with them went – yes! you've guessed it – Houdini, a mere two-year-old. They were all bought by a farmer from the Clwyd who was well pleased with the transaction. I wonder how long he stayed in that same frame of mind? Once the meadows started to grow again and Houdini had been moved to pastures new with her companion roamers, peace reigned for a while. Then Bob and Dick sold more stock and reshuffled the flock, sending most to the mountain. Some needing fattening, having suffered a little during the heat wave, went to the bottom field. Among these sheep were some of Houdini's jokers, but the river was running high and it was very unlikely that any of them would attempt to cross.

Imagine our amazement when one morning half a dozen of our sheep were grazing calmly on the other side of the raging torrent. The brothers were flabbergasted because it seemed inconceivable that any domestic animal would attempt such a crossing especially when there was plenty of food to hand. But cross they had, and were chased home by a very irate Dick, as in their interest it was thought undesirable to force them through the water once again. Sheep are subject to viral pneumonia, which is generally fatal and is caught when the animals are wet and cold; also, there was a very real chance of one of them drowning.

There was no doubt at all about how they got across, for I caught three of them next morning as they swam and battled with the current. This time there was no sentiment, back through the water they came with the dogs hard on their heels. This state of affairs carried on for several days as it was impractical just then to return those particular ewes to the mountain. But the climax came after a real humdinger of a stormy night when the river burst its banks and flooded the surrounding fields – unbelievable that five short weeks before, dried caked mud covered the area instead of this very large lake.

The majority of the sheep were on high land at the top of our pasture and were quite safe, but through the trees at the other side of this instant lake were two lambs knee-deep in water. They must have crossed the night before and got trapped. Needless to say this was the straw that broke the camel's back. Practical or not, up to the mountain that pair went. Houdini, the old master, had taught her pupils well.

While these cavortings were going on, Dilys placidly chewed her cud, sneaked into the garden whenever possible and continued her life as a privileged sheep. Her tricks continued; once in the garden she would hide herself round the back of the greenhouse, chewing contentedly at some choice morsel until chivvied back to the field. Meanwhile, Houdini's pupils were safe on the mountain – or were they?

16

Nell

She waddled from the car, her fat chubby legs quite inadequate to carry her body weight, which quivered and shook as she walked into the house, her keen puppy eyes observing every detail of our living room. Then suddenly she turned her adorable black sheepdog face and looked at me. From that moment she took her place alongside Cymro in my heart – two of my favourite dogs. I loved Cymro for his sense of fun, his sheer nerve, and the peculiar arrogance that emanated from him, but Nell was quite the cleverest dog I have ever known. Even as a puppy she would look at and sum up the situation. She too was arrogant, but in a less impersonal way, and bless her, she was capable of a very deep loyalty. As with most sheepdogs, her master was paramount. His word was law, and she was his slave.

Nell was John's all-time favourite; he relied so much on her judgement, and they were perfect together, each judging the other's mood. John's people had always been farmers, originally at Hendre Fawr and Hendre Bach. Both farms were sold – Hendre Fawr in the 1920s, and Hendre Bach during the war – but a flock of sheep was retained, shepherded by John's two cousins, Bob and Dick, and maintained on our land and some rented fields on the Sychnant Pass Road. The two cousins, however, were getting old and wanted John to help them initially and eventually take over the flock. Hence the necessity for a sheepdog. Luckily a friend living on the Lleyn Peninsula had a spare puppy and assured us that she was descended from prize stock, and indeed time would show that she was.

One big worry was car sickness. The journey from the Lleyn was punctured by numerous stops, but as our car required much cleaning, it was evident that health-wise, all was not well with the puppy. Not only was she very fat, sick and full of lodgers, but her breath smelt and she was very lethargic. In consequence John had a talk with his friend and learned that the puppy had been fed copious amounts of cake by his wife. Luckily a worm tablet, a visit to the vet, plus a healthy diet soon saw her coat shining. But the car sickness continued for some time, in spite of the fact that she became addicted to cars, and every time a car door was opened, she was there, her little face upturned, her lovely expressive eyes begging imploringly. Time took care of the sickness but her love affair with cars remained all her life.

Just up the road from our house lived a pesky sheepdog-cum-terrier, half Nell's size. To say he was amorous at certain times of the year would be an understatement, for oh! what a determined animal he was. Having decided that Nell was the bitch for him, he defied strong gates, sticks, pitchforks, barbed wire and buckets of water to carry out his courtship. Eventually two small puppies resulted, totally unlike, one black, one white. Luckily we were able to find good homes for them. In spite of this setback, Nell went on to have several sets of first-class puppies. We sold most of them, but apart from those we kept, we never heard whether they emulated Nell or possessed her keen brain.

At that time John was anxious to take early retirement, with a view to creating a small market garden as we had ample land, most of which was used by John's two cousins for sheep grazing. We had always culti-vated a vegetable plot here even when we lived at Groesffordd while John's mother lived here, but now he enlarged it and planted it with a variety of vegetables. Unfortunately we also had hens, who would constantly escape from their pen and scratch and scratch at the rows of newly planted seeds. It was a case of Nell to the rescue for she quickly understood what was required of her and had them rounded up in a trice. Just 18 months old and with no formal training, she was a joy to watch as day after day she'd repeat the task and we were rewarded in due course by a fine crop of vegetables.

Nell was a totally different animal from Cymro, a working dog totally dedicated, thoroughly loyal to the household, and not only John. Once trained she became a dog in a thousand. Several farmers suggested that she would make a good trials dog (sheepdog trials), but John was just not interested. His time was short and valuable, for at that time he was still working full-time, cultivating a large plot of land, and helping his elderly cousins with the sheep.

For a long time we only had Nell, but Bob and Dick's dogs were getting old and another dog became imperative. Dolly, one of Nell's pups, was a lovable animal, but hopeless with the sheep. She just wasn't interested. John spent hours trying to train her, but to no avail. She just became a well-treasured pet. She too had puppies and when Nell was getting on we kept one of hers, Siân, who outlived Nell.

On market and movement days, Nell seemed to know what was happening and would slip away to await John at the field gate, and would have the sheep rounded up and ready to board the livestock trailer without a word spoken or any command given.

When it became necessary to rest the home fields, the sheep were walked to their new home. Nell then became invaluable. She would stalk (no other word will describe her actions) the sheep from our house down our lane, through a large housing estate on the edge of Conwy, and out on to the Sychnant Pass Road, depositing them safely on the side grass verge by the field gate to await John, who was riding behind the flock in his little green van. This manoeuvre always took place at dawn before the inhabitants of the estate became alive, and only when a small number of sheep was involved. If a large number required moving, a longer but quieter route was used, and the whole family darted here and there shutting gates and guiding sheep past entrances where there were no gates. Nell at these times took her rightful place at the head of the column, whilst the lesser dogs chased recalcitrant sheep, nosed them from the hedgerows, and removed them from chewing prize garden plants.

When herding the sheep Nell was a martinet; heaven help the poor animal who desired a tasty morsel from a nearby shrub. A loud bark would issue, and the animal moved swiftly back to the flock before those flashing fangs could sink into her flesh. At all times Nell was ruthless with fully grown sheep, but when lambs were with the flock, she was oh! so gentle, unless of course they got frisky and decided to play. Woe betide them then.

Nell's intuition saved John many a heavy task. She would instinctively know if an animal was ill or in trouble and would run and bark until John followed her to the stricken sheep. Many's the time one of them would become enmeshed in barbed wire, or have lumps of the dangerous stuff hanging from their fleeces. She was always there, and wouldn't move until help was obtained.

Quite late in her life she was largely instrumental in saving our house from being burgled. Originally a crog loft cottage consisting of one very high, reasonably large living-room, with a bedroom alongside and another very low room above, the house is now more like a bungalow with two more rooms, a hall toilet and bathroom attached. At the time of the attempted attack I was asleep in the downstairs bedroom, alone, for John was away and Richard, our youngest son who lived with us, was out.

It was some time after midnight when I was awakened by Nell's deafening bark and heard an unmistakably female voice say, 'They are all over the place.' To say I was terrified was an understatement.

110

The voice came from outside a little window at the end of my bed; the bathroom window is alongside and it sounded as if they were trying to get in that way. I was so shocked that I sat bolt upright, but didn't put the light on. Why? I don't know; it all happened so quickly. Nell in company with Dolly and a dog we were minding kept up a high volume of noise, running backwards and forwards from room to room. There were sounds of much activity outside – footsteps, and a lot of clinking and clanking. Then that female voice shouted, 'The police are coming,' there were no more noises, just the sound of a car starting up and moving away, and another car passing.

The dogs stopped barking and blessed peaceful silence reigned. Nell moved quickly from the toilet window and padded into the bedroom, thrust her trusting dark head and sympathetic, expressive eyes into my hand, lying on the counterpane, assuring me, as if a torrent of words had been used, that she and her companions were my true protectors and friends.

Nell, apart from being a school marm to sheep and a very efficient working servant, was treated as a loving and much-loved pet. Not for her, or any of our dogs, the wet and cramped confines of an outdated kennel, like most sheepdogs. Oh no! She wallowed on soft sofas, smothered in cushions and was often seen lying on her back with a cushion to her head, luxuriating on our best sofa. Like many sheepdogs, she loved a game and swimming for sticks in the river that bounds our property.

The one dreadful habit she had was barking at every car that passed us either way. Her bark, always loud, became deafening, and car travel became a nightmare, for every time the car was even thought about, she would be there, ready to jump in. The trouble was the herding instinct. Nell, in her innocence, related every moving object to sheep, travelling cars were sheep – her sheep – and they must not pass her. John became inured to this, thankfully, because she was with him all the time, but I never became used to it and hated travelling with her, especially on a long journey.

We lost her once in 1979 when we had a wedding party in our garden for our niece. The next morning everybody turned out to help clear up, and there was a lot of movement with laughter and banter, and Nell, who disliked noisy crowds, disappeared. During the party we had closed her in a bedroom, but forgot to close her in next day. Eventually we found her a quarter of a mile away in a neighbour's garden, cowering in the shrubbery. She was shaking and shivering, but after a nice drink and much petting she was her usual dominant self.

After 16 years Nell became arthritic, her sight became very blurred, and she developed a heart condition. So it became imperative to get another dog, for Siân could not be fully relied upon and Dolly had died a few years previously. John had his eye upon a bitch about six months old who had impressed him, but I did not really want another dog. So for a time we had a stalemate situation, which ended when Nell suddenly died.

Full of grief, I was preparing the evening meal on the day of Nell's death, when I heard muted giggling outside the door, which was opened and a puppy thrust in. I looked at her quickly, and saw quite the prettiest sheepdog puppy I have ever seen. Her head was well shaped and of typical sheepdog style, her features were neat, and the fur on her face was fine and beautifully patterned in white, black and brown, but her eyes were large and very expressive. I turned away quickly and resumed my task. After half an hour of silence, I got a bit worried, wondering what she was doing, but on turning round I saw she was curled up contentedly on the sofa.

She suddenly sat up and looked at me; I melted, she was so very beautiful. 'You've made your place here, haven't you?' I said. 'Well, you'd better stay, then.' So she became another of our well-loved dogs.

We have had a succession of sheepdogs since Nell, and they were all highly strung. Topsy hated the vacuum cleaner, and as soon as she saw it emerging from the cupboard, she moved away. Spot, our current dog, hates noises and will hear a shot from a gun or a firework a mile away, pushing herself into the tiniest cranny, all the while quivering and shaking. Even a sneeze terrifies her.

When the animal economic situation got out of hand it became imperative to sell the sheep. For years there had been no profit, and John at 80 was unable to cope on his own, so we had no alternative as our two sons were too busy to even contemplate keeping them. But it was a sad day, for the Williams family at Hendre Fawr and Tyddyn Melus had kept sheep since time began.

17

The Women's Institute

In the mid-1950s the Women's Institute movement was extremely strong and new branches were springing up everywhere. Being an educational organisation, it escalated, for the young people were now being given opportunities that had been denied to the ordinary population in the past. This movement offered courses right across the board and together with the social opportunities, proved a magnet for the younger generation.

In 1959 a local very rural branch was instigated in an outlying Conwy district, and I became the first secretary. It was very successful and ran courses in dressmaking, glove-making and first aid, plus others that have escaped my memory.

Drama also was popular, and at the first Christmas show we included a human cow (one person as front legs and another as back), which was milked by a milkmaid. The milk came from a squeezy bottle manipulated by the rear actor. This, of course, brought the house down and was very popular, and over the years became a must at events throughout the locality.

Soon after we started I was chosen to represent my colleagues at the Annual General Meeting at the Albert Hall, and as I came from the Surbiton district and hadn't been home for a long time, I was agog to see my parents and brother. However, I was not only going as a delegate, for at the end of the annual proceedings a

115

'Brains Trust' panel would answer questions about the content of BBC programmes; I was to ask a question set by our branch, one of 12 picked from many. The question was, 'Why are so many violent cowboy films screened daily on *Children's Hour*?'

There was also a bonus: Mr Peter Thomas, our MP, had invited myself and the other two local delegates to tea on the terrace of the Houses of Parliament and a guided tour afterwards. This outing was a great success; the three of us enjoyed ourselves immensely.

I asked the 'Brains Trust' question without mishap. The panel replied to my question by saying that as soon as something suitable came up they would change the format. Fifty years later violence still seems to me to be at the heart of children's programmes. *Dr Who* might be good viewing, but survival by slaying seems to be the norm.

When we moved in 1975, I changed my Institute, Conwy WI being much nearer. It was also held in the afternoons and meant evenings were free to be with John. This WI was large – 110 strong with 50 on the waiting list. It was at this time that our movement fell out of favour with the young when an anniversary book was launched called *Jam and Jerusalem*. The powers-that-be thought it was an apt title, as it encompassed our love of domesticity with the wider issue of political and environmental improvement. The modern young, so different from the post-war teenagers, immediately dubbed it uncool, the words 'Jam and Jerusalem' were derided throughout the land, and membership, which had also been hit by the necessary yearly fee increase, plummeted.

This state of affairs lasted a good many years until the Yorkshire calendar girls reversed the trend. Our WI was badly affected: over a period of 30 years we lost more than a hundred members, ending up in 2007 with just nine, when sadly we closed.

In our heyday two stalwart ladies quietly and efficiently, often from the back benches, ruled our branch. Mrs Olwen Davies and

Mrs Bennett Hughes were best friends and were much loved and revered by all, but their word was law, and if they said an undertaking was against WI charity status rules, then this was immediately abandoned.

Of all our activities, dramatic art was our two ladies' favourite pastime. They were both excellent actresses and enriched our lives with their performances. Always anxious to keep a balance between the English and Welsh members, we held an annual English Day near St George's Day and a Welsh Day as close to 1st March, St David's Day, as possible.

Both entertainments were well above average quality for amateurs and delighted our guests who were drawn from neighbouring WIs. The Welsh language was the basis for the first show of the year in March with solo and choral items, plus sketches. I was always more involved in English Day because of my nationality, and I produced two or three shows. Two highlights that come to mind are a Charlie Chaplin sketch with a very talented actress taking the part of Charlie, her antics causing much amusement; and a Joyce Grenfell classic – the teacher and a class of infants. Again, the actress who played the much-tried mistress was in a class of her own. All our members were dedicated to the success of the Institute, and for many it was their only social activity. Unfortunately, the modern miss boycotted our organisation for a very long time, and that and the passing of our elderly members brought about its demise.

Membership nationwide is much more buoyant nowadays in England but is slower to revive in Wales, probably because there is a thriving sister-type Welsh language organisation. Apart from the calendar girls there was another event that helped boost our membership. Some years ago one of the last events to be held at the old Wembley Stadium was our AGM, and I was once again a lucky delegate. There were three resolutions on the agenda that year. One concerned the payments of benefits, especially elderly benefits, if local Post Offices closed. The second discussed the funding of hospices, and the third dealt with the treatment of strokes. Then Prime Minister Tony Blair was the speaker after the resolutions had been discussed, and whilst his comments were met with some disquiet, it was when he started to become party political that there was slow clapping everywhere and one or two catcalls. When the time came for any questions, delegates really made their wrath tell, for one of the WI rules is that nothing party political must be discussed at national or local level. All the papers were full of it, and the media also blazed forth; our carriage on the train home was party like, with members and travellers alike euphoric that Mr Blair had unwittingly given the WI much-needed public attention.

Some time during the 1970s, I was made group convenor, in charge of activities throughout the Conwy Valley, and I was very keen to establish a local WI Market. These markets have been prevalent since 1925, but at that time there were none in our federation. They are co-operative and give rural people, both men and women, the opportunity to earn a little extra money by making and selling quality handmade goods. However, it was not to be, as there was only one other person, a Mrs Peg Barker, who was interested in the project.

Fourteen years later Mrs Sheila Dillien, a newly arrived resident, was invited to Mrs Peg Barker's house and during conversation the hostess remarked that she had always regretted the lack of a WI Market in the valley. Back home, Sheila turned on the radio and, lo and behold, listened to a talk on – you guessed it – WI Markets.

Within a few months a market was installed every Friday in Trefriw and has been very successful for the last 20 years. In 1995 the government of the day decided that the WI was indeed a charity, but the market section did not meet the charity criteria, for each individual benefited from the sale of their articles. Therefore the market became separate, and was designated a business. The name was changed to Country Markets in 2004.

In 2004 swamping floods occurred at Trefriw, a once quite thriving large spa village situated on the banks of the River Conwy. Floods have always been a feature of the landscape here but dredging and land reinforcements had kept the river at bay until this last one, which was, like all Britain's recent floods, devastating.

Prince Charles, always alert to the problems of Wales, visited Trefriw in the summer of that year, and a special WI Market was convened for that occasion. Since my husband John had retired in 1980, we had developed our smallholding into a market garden and sent quite a lot of our resultant produce and plants to this weekly outlet. On 'The' day our three main sections, baking, craft and gardens, were laden with home produce, and we awaited the heir to the throne with much excitement.

On arrival he talked animatedly with all the stallholders, buying a fruit cake in the process. When he was introduced to me we talked of plants and gardens, both getting carried away on a pet subject. His interest and consideration for my insignificant views were remarkable, and this showed on his face. One of the photos taken by a colleague mirrors this interest, and it is one of my most treasured photographs.

After talking to me, he moved on to chat to Mrs Mary Snape, our chairman, a friend and fellow plant devotee, giving the same rapt attention to their conversation. All of a sudden he turned back and said, 'Would you ladies like to come to Highgrove?'

'Oh, yes please!' we chorused back, and true to his word, his representative got in touch with Mrs Lyn Waite, our organiser, and 25 of us travelled to Highgrove, his country home, renowned for its organic farm and gardens.

We had a memorable time there, many of the unusual features having been innovated by the Prince himself. The whole place was unique and it is quite obvious that the entire concept was developed to highlight the significance of organic methods at a time when these matters are vital for the future survival of our planet.

Prince Charles is to my mind a very caring person. The individual attention he showed to me and my friends was accorded to everyone he met that day, and if he can show this humanity to a bunch of very ordinary folk, surely this augurs well for our monarchy in the future.

18

Nooks and Crannies: A Collection of Favourite Places and Unusual Occurrences

First must come the River Thames. I played alongside this most famous river when I was a child, and I swam and canoed on it when I was older. I loved its dark dappled water lapping, lapping all the time and still do now. My happy hunting ground was both sides of the river at Surbiton and Kingston. One memorable hot summer was spent by the river at East Molesey with some young friends.

We played in the small bays with the sandy mud, paddled and sunbathed, we listened as the pleasure steamers passed by and waited for the resultant wash of water that rocked and sometimes overturned small rowing boats. We collected pebbles, shells and pieces of broken porcelain, tied them up in a hanky and buried them. We ran along the towpath and ate our sticky sandwiches with relish. Oh! halcyon days, long gone, but remembered with much pleasure.

Secondly must come the sea of gold. When my younger son was able to walk 2 or 3 miles, one Sunday we roamed the lower reaches of Tal-y-Fan, the mountain that rises dour and supreme over our little domain. We – John and I, Hugh our elder son, and toddler Richard – took a different route, one we hadn't explored before, and all of a sudden we were confronted by a sea of gold, 'a host of golden daffodils'. The whole mountainside was covered with short, double, wild daffodils.

'This must be the back of Daffodil Mountain,' I said to John, for this location was well known and for years people from the coast had traipsed past our house in cars and on foot on their way to plunder this one place that grew wild narcissus. They would return with armfuls of the precious flowers, oblivious of the harm they were causing. All this occurred before wild daffodils became a protected species.

We stood in awe; obviously few people knew about this dingle, making their way to the main site which had nowhere near as many flower heads as this fertile spot. Living a very busy life, I have never revisited that beautiful hillside, but it remains in memory.

Another favourite nook is my lovely rambling brook that babbles and crackles along the bottom of our smallholding. Kingfishers flit undeterred, a heron regards this particular reach as his kingdom, an otter paddles past occasionally, and rabbits abound on both shores. It was a bubbling trout stream when I first came here over 60 years ago, then just after the war an old lead mine was revitalised and deposited its waste into the small river, killing the trout. But about 20 years ago, with the mine long gone, my younger son Richard caught quite a large trout, and since then fish have been seen in the river – hence the heron.

My next story is also a nook in my life. About 15 years ago the whole family was assembled in our house, more by accident than design. It was a Sunday and Betty, John's sister, was visiting from Chester, and we were having a good old chinwag when John very excitedly burst open the door. 'Come outside quickly,' he said. 'Be as quiet as you can.' We all followed as silently as possible across the road and halted at the gate of one of our sloping fields. In the moonlight we beheld a sight not seen by many people. The whole meadow was covered by groups of hares, all sitting upright, some in batches of sixes and sevens, others smaller in twos and threes. Everywhere was silent, nothing moved. It was eerie, yet a time of wonderment. We stayed with them for about half an hour, then went back into the house. John returned some time later and said they had gone.

A few weeks later I watched a nature programme on the TV. Amazingly there was a sequence about hares, and the presenter said that on occasions they were wont to congregate in groups such as we had seen, and were known as 'Hares' Parliaments'.

Another natural experience occurred a few years later. Returning one late evening from a night out, we deposited the car where it lived in an old outhouse at the side of our large vegetable patch and walked slowly through the garden to the house. Suddenly the silence was broken by the sound of gnawing. John turned to me, 'Whatever is it?' We turned our steps into the direction of the sound, and in the dark we dimly made out a line of lettuces bordered by two rows of hedgehogs chewing enjoyably on the numerous snails that were devouring our next salad meal. Again the sheer wonder of it silenced us both, but we felt enriched by this quite bizarre occurrence.

A rather outlandish incident happened back in 1944. At that time I was in the WAAF at Rednal, and as Hitler was busy with the buzz-bombs, it was deemed sensible for me to spend my leave in Wales.

One day Sally, my mother-in-law, was without bread and I offered to walk the quarter mile to the village shop at Groesffordd. In those days the road was really a lane, because the grass borders and ditches took up most of the space available. The middle surface was tar-macked, but it was very narrow. Today because of the traffic the hard surface touches the hedges. Wildflowers and small animals lived happily among the grass and crickets were to be heard in the evenings. As I walked out onto the road I saw what I thought was a bundle of rags on the verge beside the cottage, but it moved. I stood still, only the birds were singing. What on earth was in that parcel of rags? A tiny, dirty but definitely adult hand appeared, then a small head. I ran and ran until I reached the shop. When I came back the apparition had gone.

When I confronted Sally with the story, she laughed and said, 'It was the old lady from Llanrwst; she's barely four feet tall but she's not a dwarf. She often sleeps there when she's down this way. After you'd gone she called as usual for some food. I always feed the tramps.'

As I have said, that was in 1944 when I was just 20, and tramps abounded in this rural area until the early 1970s. Like Sally, I always gave them food, as pennies were too scarce. The last tramp who came threw my bread and cheese into our front garden. I was annoyed and vowed not to waste my husband's hard-earned money again, but that was the last of them. I have never seen a tramp since. Nowadays they are called homeless and stick to built-up areas, and on the whole are far more tragic than the old-time country hobo.

This cranny is a comic one although I don't think the victim thought so. About 20 years ago a chap I will call Paul lived in the cottages down the road from Tyddyn Melus and rented the nearby farmyard and outbuildings. On the other side of this small farmyard there was a large house occupied by some London people who were very unused to country living. Unfortunately, Paul had a cockerel who enjoyed life and crowed perpetually, especially in the early hours. The lady, a real Cockney, complained bitterly but in vain as the neighbours laughingly told her cocks do crow and cows and bulls bellow, but that was country life, and surely the trains and buses were very noisy in London.

Nothing would placate her, and one night, or rather at four in the morning, she sent her husband in his nightshirt to complain to Paul. He knocked on Paul's door and waited. A head appeared at the window and the man protested volubly. Paul reached under the bed and pulled out the chamber pot and poured its contents over the victim's head.

There was no more grumbling, and the couple moved away soon after.

One significant incident took place before I was born, but to this day I cannot come to terms with what this woman did to my dad. Way back in 1916 Dad worked at McGriggers bank, the financial house that was responsible at that time for all the monetary dealings with serving Army officers. His occupation was reserved and he was also responsible for the upkeep of his widowed mother who was over 60 and did not enjoy good health. His brother Frank was in the Royal Navy.

One day he was looking through his post, and recognising a cousin's handwriting he opened it, and a white feather dropped out. There was no letter, just this one white, very fragile, feather. My father had had many misgivings about not entering the fray, but had been swayed by his bosses and family friends who argued that the job he was doing was equally as important as firing a rifle. And there again, how would his mother live without him? But now he dropped everything and went to the nearest recruiting centre and enlisted.

His mother confronted his cousin who freely admitted her action. She said, 'Why should my brothers fight when George had a cushy, well-paid job?' No thought had been given to the hurt that was caused by such a drastic message, or that without her son's support, her aunt would be destitute. As it happened the old lady (my dearly loved Gran) went to live with a great friend and repaid her by helping in the kitchen.

Apparently sending a white feather to young men who weren't in uniform was prevalent among young women of the day, and if there is any reader unaware of the message of the white feather, it meant, 'You're a white-livered coward, too frightened to join up.'

Hurt as he was, Dad felt that the only way out was to join the Army, so having made up his mind he was determined to succeed although he knew he had one very bad hurdle to cross. Since a child he had suffered from bad eyesight, wearing very thick lenses. The compulsory enlistment eye test had to be undertaken and passed. How? Luckily, whilst waiting, he stood by the letter board and memorized the whole set-up, so when it came to his turn he reeled off the required sequence and got an A1 pass.

Whilst in the trenches, he was buried alive by a nearby explosion but was dug out two days later. He returned to civvy street with a damaged ear that required two mastoid operations, and a groggy chest.

To the end of his days he was very hurt by that fearful message, and even though the woman is dead and buried this many a year, I will never forgive her. This is indeed a cranny I will never forget.

When I was a child living in Surbiton and Father was without a job, of necessity we shopped as cheaply as humanly possible. One Saturday morning, Mother had nothing but a few shillings to feed us for at least a week. She gave me half of it together with a priced list of items required. She bade me spend as little as possible and try to bring some change home. I was about nine at the time, and already a hardened shopper.

I made my way to Kingston Market about a mile away and had a grand time. I went from shop to shop, playing one against the other and always buying the cheapest. Totting up on Mum's prices, I found I had saved a shilling – a whole shilling! I ran the mile home. That shilling was worth £1000 to us, and my mother's smile said it all.

*   *   *

Another gem of a nook also occurred when I was even younger. I must have been about six or seven when my friends from next door, Betty and Peggy, who were about three and four years older than me, took me with them and entreated me to hurry. 'Come on, run, Mary or we will miss it.' Nobody told me where we were off to and I followed blindly, running as fast as I could to keep up with them.

Finally we stopped at the top of a grassy slope. 'It's coming now,' yelled Peggy. 'Look!' In front of us in the sky was a silver cigar-shaped object travelling majestically along. Yes! It was the R101 airship on its tragic final journey to Paris.

A similar incident happened in 1950. I was staying with my parents at Worcester Park in Surry. My second child, Hugh, was with me. He was about eleven months old and just toddling. Walking home from the nearby shops one day with Hugh in his pram, I happened to look up and saw the funniest sight. Flying high above me was an object the size of a small aeroplane, but there the resemblance ended.

This thing had no wings and consisted of pipes of varying sizes intertwined with metal couplings and numerous cogs in the shape of a square. In a flash I knew what it was: for about six months the paper and radio news had been full of a new wingless aeroplane, nicknamed 'The Flying Bedstead', that the boffins had been busy designing and building. This new phenomenon was eventually to die a natural death, being deemed uncommercial, but no doubt the inventors were very satisfied that they had created a wingless plane.

Right up to the late 1960s the telephone system here in Wales was virtually non-existent, with only the better-off possessing private phones, and public phones were few and far between. Our road is 4 miles long and ends up on Tal-y-Fan, and for years there was one phone box placed roughly halfway.

Nowadays phone communication is a must, especially for the

young, and the service has improved 100 per cent. During my early life here it was commonplace to pick up a phone and get a crossed line. Here is a funny nook that occurred just after we had the telephone installed.

After dialling the number, no one replied, but I could plainly hear two men's voices. Thinking rightly that the lines were crossed, I dialled again, only to be confronted with the same situation.

In desperation I spoke, only to hear one man say, 'Wait a minute, Mr Jones, there is a woman on the line.' Then the mystery voice spoke to me. 'Madam! Who do you think you are talking to?'

'Someone who lives in South Wales, I should think, judging by the accent,' I said.

At that he laughed; he was indeed from the south, and worked for our local labour exchange. Just another crossed line.

Another similar incident occurred after I had finished a call. Before putting the phone down, I heard a muted conversation in a farm kitchen where the phone must have been left off the hook, for a running tap could be clearly heard, as well as voices, plus the loud barking of a dog.

My last cranny is a memory. Last week, shopping in one of Tesco's palatial stores, I was transported back in time, shopping in Kingston about 1933. I remembered a small arcade just off the Apple Market and waist-high up in a wall a counter was inserted. The name 'Tesco' was placed above and a few groceries were displayed on a shelf at the back. I do not think this was the first Tesco, but it was certainly one of the earliest. We as a family shopped there regularly; the goods were cheap but of good quality. No wonder they survived. Does this make me their oldest shopper? For I have been shopping with them for roughly 76 years.

19

Rapport

When I was already over 80, someone came into my life and became one of my greatest friends, sharing my love of the written word. I cannot start her story there, however, but must go back to 1945 when my parents boarded an LMS train at Euston en route for North Wales to attend my wedding.

We had decided to hold our wedding in Conwy at the old Church in Gyffin, called St Benedict's, because all John's ancestors had been married there. Although my mother-in-law had been brought up in a very different part of Caernarfonshire, she too had agreed to hold her wedding at the old family church. I readily agreed, for we had only lived in the diocese of Guildford for four years, and for most of those I had been serving in the Air Force, and it suited my purpose to agree for I had already begun to love North Wales.

Seated in their carriage, my dad noticed an elderly, white-haired lady sitting opposite him. There were no other occupants, so he began a conversation, asking where she was bound for.

'Conwy. It's a small town in North Wales, and it is my home.'

'Oh,' replied my dad, and this was when the train had barely left Euston Station on its way to Chester, where all North Wales passengers are obliged to change trains. 'We are going there too. I have been once, but my wife has never been. Our daughter is getting married there tomorrow. It is my future son-in-law's home.'

'What a coincidence!' beamed the old lady. 'Whereabouts does he live?'

'Out in the country,' Dad answered. 'On the Hendre Road; their name is Williams.'

'My name is ordinary, too – it's Jones, and I live on the Hendre Road. I think I know the young man; is his name John?'

'Yes!,' said Dad. 'He has one sister.'

'That's right, and her name is Betty.'

Thus began a long, happy conversation which lasted all the way to Conwy, where Mrs Jones shared our taxi, for John and I met them all at the station.

Before they left Conwy my parents were invited to tea at Nant Cottage, Mrs Jones's home. This friendship continued, and when Mrs Jones's daughter-in-law Lillian (married to her son George) gave birth to two sons, one before and one after I had my son Hugh, the youngsters became firm friends. None of the three married young; my Hugh was the first when he wed Thea at the age of 35, the older Jones son, John, followed in his late forties, and his brother Peter remained a bachelor until his early fifties.

I lost my husband in 2004 and the year was a dismal one, although I am very lucky because my younger son Richard lives with and cares for me, as I am very lame due to that accident I sustained in the 1960s. Christmas, naturally, was very quiet that year but my family came to Christmas lunch as usual.

On Boxing Day Richard was out, and I was on my own when there was a knock at the door. It was Peter, Mrs Jones's grandson, and he had brought his new wife to see me. I made them welcome, and it soon became evident that this new addition to the neighbourhood and I were of the same ilk, even though she is 20 years younger than me. I began to love Sylvia from that time on. During that morning Peter mentioned that Sylvia had enjoyed reading the articles about Hendre that I had written for the *Weekly News*, and which he had saved.

'Sylvia likes to write, too, and has been keeping a detailed journal of our trips around Wales since we met in 2001,' Peter added. (A year-and-a-half after our Boxing Day introduction, they had a little book published of her writings and Peter's photographs, called *No, I Live Here*. It tells the rather bizarre story of how she, an American, came to meet and marry Peter.)

I was very intrigued to learn of her interest because for many years I had known that I had been given a talent, namely to be able to write, and had done very little to further this gift apart from the articles in the local newspaper. During our conversation I mentioned this, and said I could no longer type because of very bad arthritis in my fingers.

Sylvia jumped up and said, 'I'll do your typing for you,' and bless her, she has. I immediately started this narrative, writing by hand, and she has converted everything to a decent typewritten manuscript. This is a wonderful happening, when you realize that in the year 2000 Sylvia was in California absolutely oblivious of me, Peter, and Hendre Road. Who says there isn't an Almighty?

Last Christmas Sylvia intimated that they had a surprise Christmas present for me, and her demeanour showed excitement. So come the day, I opened their present with much wonder, but never in a million years would I have guessed what the article was. Some time ago I won a Women's Institute poetry competition with a poem entitled 'A Day in the Country', and Sylvia and Peter, both avid photographers, had printed my poem together with an appropriate photo opposite each verse, and framed it. The effect is stunning, and I was very moved; it now hangs in my living-room.

Sylvia not only types for me, she is practically an unpaid agent and holds herself ready at my beck and call. How can I ever repay her? I never can!

At times I had toyed with the idea of sending my work to a typing agency, for my fingers had sported large bumps for years. Then suddenly, out of the blue, the solution presented itself when a complete stranger from a far country, another culture, became my good Samaritan.

A Day in the Country

Through the stark dark branches of a winter tree
I saw a spear of light creep slowly upwards
Till the heavens with glorious light broke free
To court the morning ere its journey onward
Onward till that molten golden orb the sun
Paints the world with happiness and laughter gay
For the clouds alone have no sense of fun
And how so oft they mar a perfect day.

I paused to watch 'neath mountain steep
The mottled sparkling of a rock-strewn stream
When suddenly I saw a mighty salmon leap
Caught, curved in the sunlight, a peerless gleam
Of Paradise, a jewelled memory
At a pregnant time when spring is still asleep
And catkins dangle on the hazel tree
Whilst a field mouse from his lair doth creep.

Silently the peat-brown marsh pulses
To the criss-cross of insects' marching feet
Whilst the kestrel hovers ere he pounces
To claw a cowering creature from life's beat
Now as the heron flies due summer I behold
Skeins of rampant colour painted by the sun
And thin black fingers anointed with gold
Announce with pomp, that night has begun.

133

20

Christmas

Christmas, say the critics, is now humbug. Commercialism has driven all the Yuletide spirit through the window. Do we, the ordinary people, believe this when we congregate round our festive tables on 'the day' with all our family around us? We have looked forward to this very special occasion for weeks, the one bright light of a dreary time of the year, and much thought has gone into buying the right present for the right person.

Most of us never see the inside of a church from one year to the next, but I would bet on at least 70 per cent of the British population trying to live up to the Christian ideals they imbibed as children. So what, if the big conglomerates make a bomb out of Jesus? We in our way regard him as our Saviour, and on Christmas Day when all the shops are shut, we cocoon ourselves round a festive table with our loved ones.

For the last four years, since my husband died, there have been eleven people present at our own private celebration. My two sons, Richard and Hugh with his wife Thea, my daughter and son-in-law, Gwena and David, Gwena's two sons – my only grandchildren, Dewi and Robert, Robert's partner Clare, my adopted granddaughter who is as dear to me as any blood relation, and Rose and John, Clare's parents who are the same type of people as we are and fit into our family circle perfectly.

Our family home, Tyddyn Melus, is so old that it has all the right credentials for a family Christmas. The decorations are simple, just greenery, holly berries and lights. The large beam over the inglenook fireplace that dominates the room is swathed in holly and tiny electric bulbs. This is the work of my two grandsons who, like the rest of us, enjoy our particular way of celebrating this festive time.

Christmas Eve is the day of built-up excitement, when merry quips are on everyone's lips, when jostling shoppers fight for last-minute forgotten articles, when the turkey is stuffed and myriad vegetables cut ready for the pot. The house, which gets a lick and a promise most days, is cleaned to perfection; everyone congregates and gets stuck in. Because of my age I sit in the best seat, like a queen, and watch the worker bees work their magic.

Four years ago, just after John died from a heart attack, our number swelled to eleven when John and Rose moved from their native Stockton-on-Tees to Abergele to be near to their daughter. This set me a problem, for our dining table was designed for six but would hold eight at a pinch, but eleven was out of the question. Then the obvious solution hit me; we would put a large board on top. This has worked successfully every year since, and it is put in place by eager hands when the cleaning has taken place.

This preparatory day is as special to me as the holy day itself, for I love the hustle and bustle of preparation and the air of expectation everywhere. What will the presents bring? Will my son-in-law David like the huge axe I have bought him at my daughter Gwena's insistence, since he was exasperated when several small axes shattered on impact while splitting logs?

The day ends with several noggins and all disperse, most for an early night in expectation of the high jinks the following day. When I say high jinks, I do not mean the drinking and drug sessions that the young indulge in today, but the Victorian version which even our young thoroughly enjoy. Of course there is one vital ingredient that is missing for our Yuletide set up. What is that? you might say, slightly mystified. Why, children! Is Christmas real without a child? For their unbounded excitement, the huge, dilated eager eyes, full of wonderment and expectation. The three o'clock awakening, and the determination not to miss a second of this brilliant day. Yes! Children are missing, but with at least two adults who still act and enjoy special pleasures with all the verve and vitality of a child, that special spark is still discernible.

During my 80-odd years of life, I cannot remember waking up to a snow scene on Christmas Day. There was one notable year, a bit back, when snow fell during the evening and night, and on Boxing Day our beautiful smallholding was in glorious white. The sun came out and the sunbeams played tunes in the snow. Most years the weather is darkly overcast but with very little rain. This, thank goodness, doesn't darken our spirits, and when we congregate in my living room at noon ready for the meal of the year, exuberance and merriment abound.

I serve at table just what everyone likes. We do not have a turkey, but a large capon, a joint of beef, and a huge ham are cut and placed on the table, along with five or six different vegetables, numerous sauces and the sausages, the favourite food of my grandsons. All this is topped by the pudding alight with spirit, and trifle for those like me who are not pudding lovers.

Like everyone else throughout the land, we are now full and overfed, awaiting the next ritual on our agenda. Then they come, thousands of presents as there are eleven of us, and we pass them out willy-nilly. The laughter increases as the wine is poured bottle by bottle, and the paper beautiful in its mass of colour lies torn and dejected, knee-deep on the floor. The crackers join the excitement and tiny ornaments shower the table, and a small chamber pot causes more hilarity.

The first part of the day ceases at about 4 p.m. when we tidy, and my daughter and her family return to Henryd, a mile away, where they live. Our later meal is partaken at Gwena's. These days it's more or less a snack as we are all well overloaded with the best food in the land. After supper some sit and watch telly, the rest play Scrabble. Now this is not just an ordinary game; it is not really competitive, as we help one another, together making as many different combinations as possible. Laughter and merry jests intersperse conversation, and, to repeat an old adage, a happy time is had by all.

And so ends our Christmas – a pagan ceremony, you might say. The purists and the critics certainly do, but then didn't Jesus say, 'God is love'? And with so much genuine love and affection and the underlying realisation by everyone present that this is our Lord's birthday, how can this glorious day be regarded as heathen?